THE

QUARTERLY

EDITED BY

GORDON LISH

THE
QUARTERLY

8 / WINTER 1988

VINTAGE BOOKS

A DIVISION OF RANDOM HOUSE

NEW YORK

THE QUARTERLY (ISSN 0893-3103) IS EDITED BY GORDON LISH
AND IS PUBLISHED MARCH, JUNE, SEPTEMBER, AND DECEMBER
FOR $28 THE YEAR ($42 IN CANADA) BY VINTAGE BOOKS,
A DIVISION OF RANDOM HOUSE INC., 201 EAST 50TH STREET,
NEW YORK, NY 10022. APPLICATION TO MAIL AT SECOND-CLASS
POSTAGE RATES IS PENDING AT NEW YORK, NY, AND
ADDITIONAL MAILING OFFICES. SEND ORDERS AND ADDRESS
CHANGES TO THE QUARTERLY, VINTAGE BOOKS, SUBSCRIPTION
DEPARTMENT, 201 EAST 50TH STREET, FIFTEENTH FLOOR,
NEW YORK, NY 10022.
THE QUARTERLY WELCOMES THE OPPORTUNITY TO READ WORK
OF EVERY CHARACTER, AND IS ESPECIALLY CONCERNED
TO KEEP ITSELF AN OPEN FORUM. MANUSCRIPTS
MUST BE ACCOMPANIED BY THE CUSTOMARY RETURN MATERIALS,
AND SHOULD BE ADDRESSED TO THE EDITOR, THE QUARTERLY,
201 EAST 50TH STREET, NEW YORK, NY 10022. THE QUARTERLY
MAKES THE UTMOST EFFORT TO OFFER ITS RESPONSE TO
MANUSCRIPTS NO LATER THAN ONE WEEK SUBSEQUENT
TO RECEIPT. OPINIONS EXPRESSED HEREIN ARE NOT NECESSARILY
THOSE OF THE EDITOR OR OF THE PUBLISHER.

ISBN: 0-394-75937-0

DESIGN BY ANDREW ROBERTS
MANAGEMENT BY DENISE STEWART AND ELLEN F. TORRON

JUST PREVIOUS TO HIS DEATH IN DECEMBER OF 1987,
HOB BROUN SENT A POSTCARD TO THE EDITOR OF THIS MAGAZINE.
THE POSTCARD EXHIBITED A PHOTOGRAPH OF THE BASEBALL
PLAYER WHITEY LOCKMAN FIELDING A BALL. LOCKMAN IS SHOWN
WITH HIS BODY PARALLEL TO THE GROUND, HIS ARM REACHING
AS MUCH AS IT MIGHT. IT SEEMS AN IMPOSSIBLE POSTURE—
THE MAN IS FLYING, THE BALL WILL BE CAUGHT. IT WILL BE
IN ACCORDANCE WITH THE SPIRIT OF WHAT IS EXPRESSED
IN THIS PHOTOGRAPH THAT THE EDITOR OF THE QUARTERLY
WILL DETERMINE THE ANNUAL WINNER OF THE AWARD THIS MAGAZINE
IS ESTABLISHING—ACTING IN COOPERATION WITH
MR. AND MRS. HEYWOOD HALE BROUN—IN THE MEMORY OF HOB BROUN.
THE AWARD IS TO HAVE THE TITLE THE HOB BROUN PRIZE,
AND WILL BE GIVEN TO A WRITER OF FICTION WHOSE STORY
IS DRAWN FROM A YEAR'S CONTRIBUTIONS. THE HOB BROUN PRIZE
OF 1988 WILL BE ANNOUNCED IN Q9.

MANUFACTURED IN THE UNITED STATES OF AMERICA

THE QUARTERLY

---

8 / WINTER 1988

A NACE PAGE   2

JAN PENDLETON / *Five Fictions*   3

DOM LEONE / *I Do Not Have a Dog*   23

STEPHEN O'CONNOR /
What Makes You Think You Deserve This?   44

DIANE WILLIAMS / *Screaming*   49

DONALD N. UNGER / *Public Works*   51

DIANE DESANDERS /
The Light Falling Across It Just So   58

ALAN RIFKIN / *The Honor System*   65

RICK BASS / *Those Twisting Things*   76

A. R. DAVIS /
Spending the Day with Donald Trump   80

BROOKE STEVENS / *Minnows*   85

DIANE HOPKINS / *History*   89

WILLIAM FERGUSON /
The Clouds of Polonius   104

ANN BOGLE / *Fairness*   108

GEORGE ANGEL / *Manqué*   115

FREDERICK BUSCH / *Ralph the Duck*   117

ANOTHER NACE PAGE   134

KIRK NICEWONGER   135

THE QUARTERLY

DAVID BREEDEN   *143*

SUSAN D. ADAM   *147*

VICTORIA REDEL   *148*

V. L. BENNETT   *149*

ERIC PANKEY   *152*

FORREST GANDER   *153*

KATY AISENBERG   *154*

BARRY SEILER   *155*

PETER WOOD   *157*

ELIZABETH LERNER   *159*

PAUL K. SHEPHERD   *162*

SUSAN RAWLINS   *164*

ELAINE EQUI   *165*

JOAN KINCAID   *166*

EILEEN HENNESSY   *167*

MAURICE EIDELSBERG   *170*

M. D. STEIN   *171*

ONE MORE NACE PAGE   *174*

CYNTHIA OZICK *to* Q   *175*

THOMAS LYNCH *to* Q   *182*

VICTOR BARALL *to* Q   *193*

PETER COLE *to* Q   212

MARK JAY MIRSKY *to* Q   220

ALAN SCHWARTZ *to* Q   228

SHARON KORSHAK *to* Q   233

PAULETTE JILES *to* Q   235

CARL SPECTOR *to* Q   240

RICHARD PLOETZ *to* Q   242

EILEEN HENNESSY *to* Q   246

THE LAST NACE PAGE   248

THE
QUARTERLY

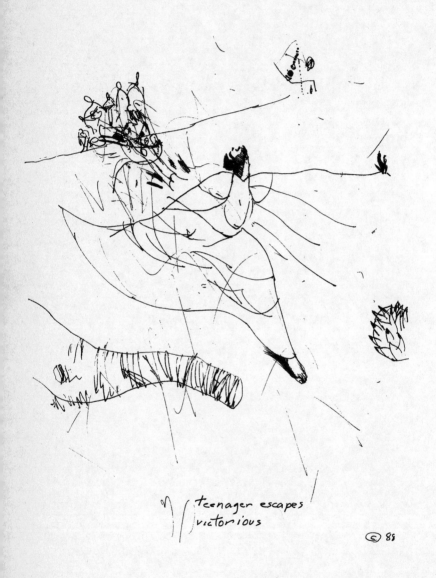

teenager escapes
victorious

© 88

The Hunter

Lydia and Jason appear to be two skeletons to Seth as they pass through the light from the window. To Seth, Lydia and Jason look like skeletons, or like brittle birds, with their long thin necks and their hair cut short, with bits of scalp showing through. Lydia sits down on the couch and she starts nursing Jason, and Seth feels sleepy or like fucking, but mostly watching Jason suck on Lydia's breast makes Seth want to sleep.

When Jason was tiny, Lydia cradled Seth in her arms and Lydia let Seth suck the milk from each of her breasts, as if Seth were Lydia's baby. Lydia's milk was sweet and thin, and later, when there was new milk, Lydia expressed her thin gray milk into bottles for Jason, and Seth worried that Lydia's milk would not be enough.

Seth leans across the couch and he kisses the small, cool mouths of Lydia and Jason, and Seth can taste the medicine that Lydia and Jason have been taking. Lydia goes to the kitchen, where she puts Jason down, and she reaches for something from the cupboard. Lydia feeds Jason orange baby aspirins and she takes a Bufferin.

"Let's go to the park," Seth says. "It stopped raining."

"Jason has an earache," Lydia says.

"He could wear his cap," Seth says.

In the park, Seth pushes Jason back and forth on the swing and Seth watches Jason's pale, chapped face between the flaps of Jason's cap. Jason squints and he blinks his eyes and Seth cannot tell if the wind pleases Jason, or if anything pleases Jason. Jason sits stiffly in the swing, looking as if he does not want to go faster or go slower, and not lifting his legs in the air. When Seth pushes Jason forward, Seth imagines the swing coming back empty.

Lydia stands to the side of Seth and behind Jason.

"June wants to have a baby," Lydia says.

Seth thinks that Lydia sounds envious at the thought of her sister having a baby. Seth imagines June growing rosy and robust, with her large breasts and her sturdy brown legs. June will smell the way pregnant women smell and she will fill the apartment with her pregnant smell.

"Who cares if June doesn't get married in order to have a baby? I don't care, do you care?" Lydia says. Suddenly Seth hates the thought of June marrying someone and moving away. June's rhythm is different from Lydia's. Lydia, Seth, and June move around each other a certain way.

When Lydia and Seth take Jason back to the apartment, June is standing in the kitchen, rocking back and forth on her bare feet, and Seth can tell that June is talking to a man. After June hangs up, Seth thinks that June will tell Seth and Lydia about the man. Seth imagines June wearing her cutoffs and holding a large bamboo-colored baby on her hip.

Seth fixes Lydia a cup of tea to help Lydia's milk come. Lydia puts Jason to her breast and Jason sucks patiently, waiting. June hangs up the phone and she comes into the living room, and Seth can smell June's shampoo, fruity, like different kinds of fruit mixed together.

"Richard is a lawyer," June says. "He tells me about his cases. Richard would be a good father, except that he has those women's hips you see on men sometimes," June says. "Did Lydia tell you I want to have a baby?"

June gets up from the couch and she leaves the room. Then she calls to Lydia and to Seth from the bathroom.

"I won't mooch off you!" June says. "I'll get a job!"

Jason has finished with one of Lydia's breasts. Lydia turns Jason around and she wipes the milk from his chin before she lets Jason find her other breast.

"Where's the Modess?" June calls from the bathroom.

"We're out," Lydia says. Lydia looks at Seth and she waits for Seth to offer to go to the store.

"Modess Supers, or Nighttimes, or whatever," June says.

Seth drives to the Safeway, thinking about living with women, how one day there is nothing left of the man.

In the middle of the night, Seth hears Lydia screaming to him from Jason's bedroom. Seth runs to Jason's room and he sees Lydia holding Jason upside down and shaking him. Jason is turning a color and he is opening and closing his fists.

Seth takes Jason from Lydia. He holds Jason by his feet and he pounds on Jason's back.

"I found him like this," Lydia says.

Lydia sounds guilty to Seth, as if Lydia is thinking the same thing that Seth is thinking, thinking about not having to push Jason in the swing and not having to watch Jason's pale uninteresting face between the flaps of his cap.

Seth reaches inside Jason's mouth, but he cannot quite reach the thing that Jason is choking on. June comes to the doorway in her striped man's shirt.

"I called an ambulance," June says.

Seth picks up a toy kaleidoscope from inside Jason's crib, and when he shakes it, silver rings fall onto Jason's blanket. June brings their coats and Seth drives to the hospital.

Lydia and Jason sit in the front seat and June leans over from the back and she pushes on Jason's chest, the way she has seen it done. Jason opens and closes his fists and he makes a gurgling sound.

"Where's the fucking hospital?" Seth says.

"Straight down, then left at the light," June says.

June sounds smooth and calm, and Seth thinks that June is only pretending to be involved. Seth pulls into the emergency circle and he runs to open the door for Lydia and Jason. A nurse takes Jason to the back of the emergency room, and Seth tells the nurse about the silver rings.

Sitting in his chair between Lydia and June in the waiting area, Seth thinks that he should be standing or walking or smoking a cigarette, instead of sitting without moving and listening to Lydia's sound.

The doctor comes to the waiting room and tells them that he has removed the ring from Jason's throat. The doctor looks at June and June lifts her fine brown hair off her shoulders.

Seth drives home through the city, feeling smug as he looks at the houses that they pass, and he thinks that Lydia, June, and he have all been called from their beds like children, and that they are the only ones who will have known this night.

"I want you both to know that I know," Lydia says. "I didn't know when it happened. But I figured it out after," Lydia says.

Seth hears June swallow. Seth thinks about June and about getting up to go to the bathroom in the middle of the night, about bumping hands with June in the hall and holding on to June's hand, and walking with June into June's room, and slow-fucking June so the springs in June's bed will not wake Lydia.

Lydia brings Jason onto the patio and she calls inside to June.

"Come have something with us?" Lydia says.

June comes onto the patio with her book and she stands looking at Jason. Seth thinks that, perhaps, taking care of Jason means that they all love Jason.

Lydia balances Jason on her hip while she pours coffee for everyone, and Seth loves Lydia for her efficiency after the night they have had.

Lydia sits at the table and she lifts her sweater for Jason, and Jason sucks on Lydia's breast. Jason is wearing his red and black cap with flaps over the ears, and Seth thinks that his son looks like a hunter who is waiting in the snow. **Q**

Widows

The man who was Dave and who was my mother's husband sat at the kitchen table eating a stack of sandwiches and looking at my mother's backside. My mother was doing something at the sink and she was wearing the brown dress she wore.

"Go coil the hose, Frank," my mother said to me. My mother did not turn around. I did not get up.

"The hose, Frank," my mother said. My mother pointed to the door with the hand that had soap dripping off it.

"Not till he stops looking at your backside," I said. I kept looking at the floor around where my mother was standing, and I did not look at my mother or at Dave.

My mother turned all the way around, holding her neck straight like a bird's neck. Then my mother started walking toward me, carrying her wet hands out in front. My mother stopped in front of me and she stood looking at me. When I looked up at my mother, I saw that my mother's skin was the color of rubber bands.

Dave stood up and he started walking around the kitchen, around my mother and back to me, and then he started walking around us again. After Dave finished walking around the kitchen, he walked back to me and he turned around and bent his knees so his backside was in front of my face.

"Feel of my ass," Dave said.

I did not move.

From where I sat behind Dave, I could no longer see my mother. Dave reached around and he picked up my hand and he put it on his ass.

"What does it feel like?" Dave said.

"Smells like a rotten sewer, sir," I said. My mother made a small, high sound, like something disappearing behind a hill.

"I don't remember asking you what my ass smelled like," Dave said. "I asked you to tell me what it felt like." With the hand that was not holding on to my hand, Dave started unbuckling his belt.

"I asked you what my ass felt like, because when I get through with you, you're not gonna feel your own ass or anybody else's ass for weeks."

Dave pulled me up from the chair and he led me to the kitchen door. When we passed by my mother, my mother started to say something, then she stopped. Dave pulled me outside and around back to the garage. Dave opened the garage door and we went inside.

"There's widows in here," I told Dave when Dave and I were inside the garage with the garage door closed.

"Widows, huh? Well, that's good, so we can be quick," Dave said.

Dave pushed me down on top of an old chair and I lay over the chair, waiting for Dave to start whipping me with his belt—hot then cold was how I thought Dave's belt would feel before it left bloody marks like train tracks across my back. I lay over the chair, waiting for Dave to hit me. Then I heard Dave start to snivel and say things from where he was standing, behind me. I could not understand the things Dave was saying, because Dave was crying and blowing his nose and talking nonsense to someone besides me inside the garage. I lay there waiting for Dave to stop crying, because I did not want to see what Dave's face looked like.

I waited until Dave was quiet, and then I got up from the chair without looking at Dave and I walked back inside the house, past my mother, who was sitting at the window, smoking her cigarette. My mother liked to sit at the window, smoking her cigarette and waiting for something to happen. The things my mother waited for did not seem to have anything to do with me or with Dave, or even with my mother herself.

Sometimes my mother held things in her lap while she waited—the cat or a bag of mending. My mother never sewed the clothes inside the bag. She just held the clothes in her lap as if they were the cat.

Dave stayed with us for a while and he followed my mother around like a dog. Sometimes Dave walked alongside my mother, and it looked as if Dave and my mother both thought of going into the other room at exactly the same time.

Every night when it was time for me to go to bed, I stood behind my mother at the window and I waited for my mother to turn her head. Then my mother would turn her head half-way around and I would kiss my mother's cheek. When I kissed my mother's cheek, I could see that my mother's face kept changing. One time, my mother's eyes looked like the eyes of the cat.

Sitting in front of the window, my mother looked like a young girl to me, or like an old woman who was sitting in the snow. Sometimes when I kissed my mother, my mother looked like someone from another town. **Q**

In the North

Lately, I had been thinking about being a priest like my father, before my father married my mother. I did not fit at S.F. State or at the store where I bagged, I did not have a girl, and the only rush I got was at church, where I could feel Jesus coming on so big He nearly blew my head off. Even after church, I kept feeling the feeling of Jesus inside me, in the middle of my belly, up and out through the top of my head. When I went to class, all I could think about was Jesus, about the buzz of Jesus, the way Jesus smelled and the feel of Jesus's breath on my skin. I kept thinking about Jesus so much that I started forgetting about everything else. One time, I walked all the way home from campus before I realized that I had forgotten my bike, that I had left my bike in front of the gym.

The woman I lived with started worrying about me, the way I kept forgetting things and the things I said to Jesus, and one night Sandra (pronounced Sondra) slipped a piece of paper under my door with a number written on it. When I called the number in the morning, a woman answered from the county mental health services. I went to see a shrink a few times to please Sandra, but the shrink could not relate, no more than Sandra could relate. The sad part was that I knew if these people would quit their yapping for a solid minute, they would be able to feel Him, too, the shot of Jesus that rips through your belly. But you couldn't tell people a goddamn thing. Sometimes when I woke up in the morning, I would have dark circles under my eyes like I had not slept, and I knew Jesus had been there with me all night.

The only other thing I think about when I am not thinking about Jesus is I think about numbers. About how numbers fit together and the patterns numbers make, the primes and the divisibles, and how numbers, like everything else, all end up relating to Jesus in the end. Instead of going to class, I take off on my bike and I start thinking about numbers. I throw a few random numbers out, like say, 3, 22, and 87, as if numbers are just numbers that do not have anything to do with each other. Then I add a few numbers to the numbers I already have inside my head while I'm riding on my bike and listening to myself breathing, and then it hits me in the gut, the pattern, the way the numbers all start falling together and forming one big fat Jesus Christ right there in front of me, grinning.

When I stop thinking about numbers and how numbers fit together, it is dark or nearly dark and I am out on the bay lands next to the water on my bike, and I think that it is the mosquitoes biting my neck which have made me stop thinking about numbers and about how numbers and Jesus come together. If I am not out on the bay lands when I come back from thinking about numbers, I am in some other city and I have to ride to a gas station and ask the attendant how to get back to Sandra's. Sometimes I think about zero. I think it was in China, or Africa, or Arabia where zeros started, and I think about numbers before there were zeros.

When my father and mother got a divorce, my father was the only one in our family who stopped going to church. There is a photograph of my mother and father just before they got a divorce, standing in front of our house, with my mother in a white blouse and a black skirt and my father in a gray suit, looking as if this is the only time my father has ever worn a suit, and as if my mother and father thought they should take a photograph of themselves in their good clothes before they divorced.

I go to church more than my mother or my twin sister, and sometimes I think that my mother and sister only go to church to please me. The last time we went to church together, my sister and I were at different universities and my mother drove up from L.A. without her husband, although I think my stepfather would have liked to come along if my mother had asked him to drive up with her. My mother, my sister, and I went to

Mass together, then we stopped at Lucky's to buy food for Thanksgiving dinner. We cooked a turkey in the kitchen of the place my sister was renting near campus, in the pans my sister borrowed from her neighbors. It was the middle of May and it was hot. We still planned to get together at Thanksgiving—having Thanksgiving dinner in May was just something my sister thought of.

My stepfather is the head of the Drama Department at the private school my sister and I graduated from, and at our Thanksgiving dinner in May, my mother told my sister and me that she planned to divorce my stepfather after the holidays. My mother said that Clayt, the name we called my stepfather, had come into our lives for a reason, and that now that my sister and I were grown, it was time for my mother to do something else.

"Clayt still hasn't written his screenplay," my mother said, as if this was supposed to explain everything.

Clayt wrote musicals for the Drama Department, and he told his students at the beginning of the semester that he was writing a screenplay and that he only planned to teach high school for a while. The way my mother and Clayt got together was Clayt chose me for the lead in one of his musicals, which he called *Sometimes You Just Can't Win,* at the beginning of my sophomore year, and my mother started helping with the rehearsals. My sister and I sang like birds and we made Clayt's musicals sound halfway decent, and I kept thinking all the way through the finale, when we all ran out on stage and held each other's clammy hands, that my sister and I were probably the best thing that would ever happen to Clayt. My sister has this very thin soprano voice, and when she sings, you would think the sound my sister makes is coming from somewhere far off, like maybe from the sky. My sister and I starred in all of Clayt's musicals, until Clayt married my mother and the principal told Clayt that he could not choose my sister or me for his leads anymore.

Before my mother married my stepfather, my mother took

my sister and me on trips that were educational. Usually, we went camping with the nature books my mother bought us at Christmas, and that she put under the tree with tags that said the gifts were from Ms. Claus, or from our dog, or from the angelfish. My mother never said any of the gifts were from her. Where we camped, there were always more plants than there were animals, so our plant book was the first to wear out. My mother bought us a new book at Christmas, along with a *Family World Atlas* and a map of the world that my mother matted and hung on the wall in the living room while we were sleeping, instead of hanging stockings.

Two summers in a row, my mother, my sister, and I drove to Canada, and we checked off the trees in our tree book that we saw on the way to Vancouver. At Yosemite, we checked off lodgepole pines and coulter pines. In Oregon, we checked vine maple, honey locust, and Northern catalpa. Farther north, we saw mountain hemlock, subalpine fir, and Western red cedar. In the book, my sister and I initialed and dated the trees we checked off, so we could look back and remember who saw what.

"I'm leaving S.F. State," I told Sandra one morning when Sandra was sitting at the kitchen table paying bills.

"I know," Sandra said. "Someone phoned. I want to give you a going-away party. I need a list of names."

"I don't have a list of names," I said.

"Then I'll invite some people from my work," Sandra said.

On the day of the party, I helped Sandra make popcorn and we set little plates of food around the living room. While we waited for people to come to the party, Sandra and I played table tennis in the garage. Then we started reading *The Glass Menagerie.* I read the part of Tom Wingfield, and Sandra read the parts of Amanda Wingfield and Laura Wingfield. Sandra and I did not think we would get far enough into the play to worry about who would read the other part, but no one ended up coming to the party, so I read the part of Jim O'Connor.

In the morning, we picked up the plates of food and Sandra drove me to the bus station. I forgot my parka, so we had to go back to the house, and when we got back to the bus station, the bus was loaded and ready to leave. Sandra stayed inside the car and I ran to catch my bus, and when I got inside, there were no seats next to the window, so I could not wave to Sandra. I looked across the aisle and I could see Sandra's car underneath the chin of a man who was sitting on the bus. Sandra's windows were smoked up from the heater, and Sandra's windows made me think about how cold it would be where I was going, in the North. **Q**

Killing the Goats

Before we moved to the goat lady's house, the goat lady lived in our house with her goats. People told us that the goat lady had more than twenty goats, and that she let the goats stay inside her house and sleep in her bed. We kept finding little silver keys that the goat lady hid in the house and in the garage. Someone said that before she died, the goat lady buried her money inside a tin case, and that one of the silver keys was the key to the case that had the money in it.

After my grandmother came to live with us, she fell on the floor and she broke her hip. I did not know until I came home and found my grandmother lying on the kitchen floor and talking to me the way she did, as if I had been there all day and my grandmother was finishing saying something that she had started saying before.

"So Charles came inside with something from school," my grandmother said to me in the slow, careful way that she said things, "and when Charles saw me lying on the floor, he sat down next to me and he kept on talking, like nothing was any different."

"Are you in pain?" I said.

"You try it and see," my grandmother said.

My grandmother kept herself very clean, and after a while, we forgot that my grandmother was always in her bed in the middle of our living room, or that my grandmother had not always been there in her bed, even when she could walk. When I brought someone home, we sat on the foot of my grandmother's bed, drinking coffee with my grandmother.

"You crumble up and blow away," my grandmother said to whoever was sitting on her bed with me. "First your eyes and your teeth go, then your bones fall out."

I did not think anyone would want to marry me, with

Charles and with a grandmother who stayed in her bed in the living room, but I brought men home sometimes, thinking that you never know for sure how people will feel about a given thing. When Charles brought his friends home, Charles and his friends started off playing in the bedroom that Charles and I shared. Then they brought their things into the living room, and Charles and his friends spread their toys out on top of my grandmother's bed. Sometimes my grandmother helped Charles put puzzles together, and I thought about Charles growing up and bringing girls home, and about the things my grandmother would say.

I started dating a man named Bennie, who drove a Spring Mountain water truck, and the first time Bennie came to dinner, my grandmother told me how to cook things for Bennie from her bed.

"Put a tablespoon full of sugar in everything, even in the vegetables," my grandmother said. "Men like sugar."

Before Bennie came, I helped my grandmother wash her hair by holding a bucket of water in back of the bed and lowering my grandmother's head into the bucket. We spread newspapers out on top of the bed so the bed would not get wet, but water splashed on the pillows. I thought my grandmother would be angry, but she just turned the pillows around and told me to get the hair dryer, the same way my grandmother put runt kittens in the oven, and if the kittens lived, my grandmother held them in front of her mouth and she breathed her hot breath on them. If the kittens died, my grandmother tossed them outside in the garbage, without wrapping them up first in a rag. One night, after Bennie had gone, my grandmother called to me from her bed.

"He's short, but I'd marry him," my grandmother said. "We can't go on living here, in a house that had goats in it."

Bennie and I were married in Bennie's parents' front yard, and when Charles and I were leaving for the wedding, my grandmother switched on the television with the little box that she held in her hands. My grandmother held on to the box the way she held on to the things that belonged to her, with her hands crossed over the top of the thing she was holding.

"Bring me a piece of wedding cake," my grandmother said.

Everyone in Bennie's family was small, and I had to bend over to kiss Bennie. I was glad Bennie was not as short as his sister was. At forty, Bennie's sister was the size of Charles. Bennie's father had red cheeks, and he kept following me around the house and showing me photographs that he had in his pocket of Bennie when Bennie was a baby. In one picture, Bennie was standing in front of someone's brown legs, and he had taken off his diaper and was holding it out in front. I kept thinking about sleeping with Bennie and how, if Bennie's feet were down there with mine, the top of Bennie's head would come about to the top of my shoulder.

Bennie's sister stayed with my grandmother, so Bennie and I could drive to Hot Springs for our honeymoon, and on the way up the mountain, Bennie told me about the different kinds of bottled water, about how you are sometimes better off drinking tap water than you are drinking bottled water.

After our honeymoon, we moved to an apartment in town. Bennie and I lifted everything but the refrigerator over the top of my grandmother's bed, and then we called an ambulance to move my grandmother. It was a cold day and my grandmother wore the coat she wore when she could still walk, and when the men carried my grandmother out of the ambulance, my grandmother made them carry her all around the yard so that she could see what the place looked like from the outside.

The apartment was a two-bedroom with a dining room, which is where we put my grandmother's bed, in the dining room, with a curtain across the front that my grandmother could open and close with a string that my grandmother kept tied around her wrist. Sometimes I think my grandmother opened and closed the curtain for no reason, just to have something to do.

Bennie went to work early, and when I came home in the afternoon from teaching, Bennie and my grandmother would be sitting on my grandmother's bed watching television. Sometimes Charles was sitting on the bed with them. I would start dinner and my grandmother would tell me from her bed how to cook the things that she liked. One time, when Charles was sitting on my grandmother's bed with my grandmother and with Bennie, I went to the bed and I lifted Charles up as if Charles were a bag of old clothes. Then I carried Charles into the kitchen and I made him sit on a stool while I cooked. I could not tell anyone, not even Charles, why I did it. After my grandmother had finished her dinner and I had taken away her tray and turned my grandmother on her side, my grandmother said something that sounded like "Count the days, Girlie."

I took my grandmother's tray into the kitchen and I started rinsing the dishes. Then Bennie came into the kitchen and he stood behind me, watching me, the way Bennie watched while I worked in the kitchen. I thought about my grandmother and about the goat lady, and about the goat lady dying before her goats had died. I thought that after the goat lady had died that someone had probably come to the house, and that someone had probably killed all the goats that were there.

One by one. **Q**

Black Flowers

I can tell that I am getting better, because I do not squirm as much when my husband comes here and tries to hold me. I used to rock back and forth on my knees and squirm around and make a squeaking or a squealing noise when my husband would try to hold me. Rocking back and forth on my knees and making the sound is how my husband said it was from the outside, but the way it felt on the inside when my husband tried to hold me was different.

One of the nurses at the hospital has a little blue cap that she wears on the back of her head, fastened to her hair in back with hairpins. The nurses do not have to wear their caps, the other nurses do not wear their caps. Only this one nurse always wears her little blue cap fastened onto her hair in back.

There is a man here who has hair on his chest so thick it looks like a forest, and I keep seeing the man's chest curling up and burning in my sleep. When I am sleeping, people come with hoses and the people try to put out the fire on the man's chest, but the man laughs at the people and then he blows on his chest to make the fire burn faster.

The woman next door has grown children who visit her, and when the woman's grown daughter visits, the daughter files all of her fingernails. The daughter starts filing her little fingernails first, and she works backward until she gets to her thumbs. When the woman's daughter leaves the hospital, all the daughter's nails are polished a different color, and we can all smell the smell of the nail polish in the morning when we wake up.

One of my doctors is young, but the other doctor is not. The young doctor and the old doctor talk back and forth to each other, and they talk to me and tell me things about the way I am. The doctors say I am getting stronger every day. When my doctors say I am getting stronger, I think they mean to say that I am getting fatter or smaller, or that I am going to die.

My mother sends me pots with violets in them and I give the violets away. Sometimes I write letters to people, but I do not mail the letters. In my letters I say things about the hospital, and about the people inside the hospital, and about the doctors. One doctor turned off the lights and he pretended that he was going to examine me, but the doctor looked inside my eyes instead, with a little flashlight that was the size of the doctor's thumb.

When I was a child, my father lived next to the theater in a cold room with a high bed, and I used to visit my father in that room. Sometimes my father and I got to sit in the living room with the old man and the old woman who lived in the rest of the house. The old woman took out a black bowl of hard candies wrapped in plastic and she held the bowl of candy in front of me. When I tried to decide which candy I wanted, my father reached under his arm so the woman would not see his hand and my father pinched me. When my father pinched me, his fingers felt like a snake.

In the morning, the old woman cooked bacon and eggs for my father and me, and we chose little boxes of cereal. When I tried to decide which cereal I wanted, my father reached under the table and he pinched my leg. After breakfast, my father went to work and I sneaked back into the man and woman's living room, where the big furniture was, and I licked the smooth things that were there. First I licked the base of the big blue lamp. Then I licked the black bowl where the woman had put the candy. When I finished licking everything in the room that was smooth, I went back to my father's bedroom, which smelled like my father, and I waited for my father to come home from working inside the theater.

. . .

A teenage boy comes to the hospital on Thursday nights and he plays the guitar. Sometimes the boy eats dinner here with us before he plays his songs, and sometimes the boy brings his girlfriend with him, a thin-boned girl with braces who wears a bracelet that has gold bears hanging from it.

I do not know what happened to my bathrobe, which I packed in my suitcase when my husband drove me here to the hospital. The nurse keeps saying she is looking for my bathrobe, but she does not find it. I think that my bathrobe will be inside my closet next to the door of my room when I am ready to leave the hospital, and that my slippers will be on the floor underneath my bathrobe, as if there is a person inside my clothes. When I was a child, our housekeeper used to hang my clothes on a hanger at the foot of my bed, and at night a woman came and got inside my clothes, and then the woman laughed at me, hanging in front of me from inside my clothes.

The nurse with the blue cap has a photograph that she carries around inside the pocket of her uniform. One time, the nurse showed me the photograph, and it was a photograph of a castle on a green hill. At the bottom of the hill there were three white dogs. The nurse said that the dogs were the reason that she carried the photograph around inside her pocket, as if I was about to ask the nurse why she carried the photograph. That is the only time I remember the nurse with the blue cap talking to anyone inside the hospital.

Sometimes I get dressed and I walk down the hallway past the nurses and past all the other rooms. On the walls of the hallway there are pictures that children draw of men and women with large heads and no feet, or with feet but no hands. There is a girl here who only draws black flowers.

One time my aunt visited me, and my aunt and I ate all of my aunt's Certs, because there was nothing to talk about. Instead of saying things to each other, my aunt and I kept eating Certs from the roll that my aunt kept in her lap, and when she left, my aunt shook my hand with the hand of hers that had the empty Certs wrapper in it.

Before I came to the hospital and before I knew my husband, a boy used to come to my house when my mother was at work and the boy would ride on me. The boy wore bell-bottomed jeans and he lifted up my skirt and he rode on me until I was black-and-blue. While the boy was riding on me, he kept his mouth over my mouth, and the boy's saliva ran down my cheeks and into my ears. After the boy stopped riding on me and went home, I looked in the mirror and there were white teeth marks around the outside of my lips, where I would have a mustache or beard if I were a man.

One time, the boy asked me to go to a party, and we double-dated with his friend. The boy's friend drove us to the drive-in movies instead of to a party like he said, and then the friend pushed his date down on the front seat and he rode on top of the girl. I felt sorry for the girl, because the girl was wearing a formal and she had a small lavender fan in her hair. When the boy rode on top of the girl in the front seat, the girl's petticoats made a rustling noise, as if the girl's petticoats thought that they were dancing. **Q**

I Do Not Have a Dog

He rinsed a cereal bowl with hot water. This was the way he had to do it now, one thing at a time. This was the way everyone had to do it. A cup. A fork. A can opener. The bowl he was rinsing was yellow with white stripes, something Cathy had found in her parents' garage. He wondered what she'd been looking for out there with the stacks of newspapers and the old tires. He also wondered how he'd ended up with this bowl. He was drying it with a paper towel when the telephone rang. He set the bowl upside down on the counter.

The telephone was on the floor. Paul Hoffman leaned over. "Hello?" he said.

"Hello," said a man's voice on the other end. "I'm looking for P. Hoffman."

"Pete Hoffman?" said Paul Hoffman. "There's no Pete Hoffman here." He cleared his throat. "But my name is Paul Hoffman. Who's this?"

"Come and get your dog," said the man. "My name is Kirk. Larry Kirk. And your dog is here, at my house."

"I don't have a dog," said Paul Hoffman. "I'm sorry," he said, and hung up the phone.

He and Cathy once had a dog. They got it when they were first married, and they kept it for five years. But this couldn't be that dog. That dog wasn't around anymore.

The phone was ringing again. Paul Hoffman picked it up. "Hello," he said.

"This is Larry Kirk," the man said. "You do have a dog, and he's here in my yard. I can hear him out there right now."

Paul Hoffman didn't say anything. Larry Kirk. For an instant Paul Hoffman wondered if there was any way he could own a dog and not realize it.

"Better come and get him," said Larry Kirk. "I'm about to

start using physical force. That's just about the only way they understand. Know what I mean?"

Paul Hoffman was staring at a calendar he had taped to the side of the refrigerator. It was the kind of calendar that had the same photograph at the top no matter what month it was.

"The thing is," said Larry Kirk, "he runs away if I chase him, but then he keeps coming back."

The photograph on the calendar was of the Grand Canyon. Paul Hoffman could see little people leaning against the railing, trying to see to the bottom. One couple was facing the other way. The woman was getting ready to take a picture. The man was wearing a bright shirt. Paul Hoffman couldn't make out their faces, but the woman seemed to be having some trouble with the camera, and the man seemed to be wishing he knew what to tell her. Paul Hoffman looked at the day's date. Saturday, March 30. He'd written a word on that space: *Rent.*

"It's a black dog," said Larry Kirk. "With white feet. What can I call him if I want him to listen?"

"I told you," Paul Hoffman said. "I don't own a dog." It was just past 3:30. He tried to think of a way to put the discussion to rest. "What kind of a dog is it?" he asked.

"I don't know," said Larry Kirk. "Like I said, he's mostly black, and he has long hair. I know what he's doing here. He came to see my Sophie. She's in heat. She's a house dog, but sometimes I take her outside. After all, she has to run. She likes to chase the neighbor kids, and they run from her, too—she's a German shepherd. But I'm not sending her out with him there. I mean, I understand how he feels. I get the same way sometimes, and I'm sure you do, too. But we know how to control it, even though it's a very natural thing. But I don't want any puppies, and I'm not cleaning up after him. So my point is, you better come over here and get him. Listen, I'm sure he's a good dog. I just don't like him near my house."

Paul Hoffman wondered what it would be like to have a dog again. It'd be nice to come home and have someone realize it. The dog he and Cathy once had used to stand on its hind legs and wave its paws. It waved and waved and waved until you were almost afraid it would stay like that forever. Then it would stop.

"So anyway," said Larry Kirk, "I'm at 171 Bradley, which is off Shennelton. I got the number tacked up to a tree out front." He paused. "You know where the light is on Shennelton? Near the real-estate place? There's a real-estate place up there. I can't think of the name of it, but it's a yellow building—"

"But I do not have a dog," said Paul Hoffman. "Do you understand?"

"Listen," said Larry Kirk. "I don't know what kind of a game you're trying to play here, but it's not that simple. Your dog is still out there, so come over and get him. That's all I'm saying."

Paul Hoffman heard barking in the background. He guessed it was probably Sophie. Only it sounded so faint he thought maybe it was his own dog he was hearing. But he didn't have a dog.

"Look," he said, scratching his shoulder. "I'll be right over."

"All right," said Larry Kirk. "Now we're getting somewhere."

Paul Hoffman put the receiver back on the hook. Then he lifted it off and set it next to the phone. He went over to the window. He slid his palms under the frame and pushed up. Down on the street, a boy was learning to ride a bicycle. He was just starting to get the hang of it, swerving into a driveway and onto the sidewalk. He coasted past a few houses, then he swung out into the street. A woman was behind him, running. Her coat was open. Paul Hoffman was pushing up on the window. Larry Kirk's voice was still in his ears. Paul Hoffman's arms were shaking from the pressure, but the window wouldn't budge. He knew he didn't have a dog anymore.

. . .

Larry Kirk was lying on his side of the bed. It was almost midnight. His shoes were on. "It's on my property," he said, into the telephone. "It's his dog, Mike, but it's on my property."

He turned over when Sharon came into the room. She was wearing eyeglasses with large blue frames.

"No, Mike," said Larry Kirk. "I don't consider that an advantage. What? No, listen."

Sharon went over to the dresser and turned on the radio. Then she sat on the edge of the bed and pulled off her shirt. She had another shirt on underneath.

Larry Kirk looked at the back of her head. "Well, who's responsible, then?" he asked. "Look, I just want to get some control over it. It's got nothing. . . . No. No, now listen." He pushed one of his shoes off. "Mike," he said, "I'm talking about getting her to sit on something. A piece of plywood, maybe, or a towel. Better yet, I could use something that already has her scent. I'm telling you, that's all it would take. That would do it."

Someone on the radio laughed. It was the host of a call-in program. "That's beautiful," he said, still laughing. "Now, let me get this straight: you interpret the sounds of animals?"

"That's right," said the caller. "What's so funny about that?"

Larry Kirk put his shoe back on and stood up.

"What are you doing now?" asked Sharon. "That dog's been gone for a few minutes. Why don't you just forget about it?"

"I already forgot about it," he said. "I just have to go downstairs for a second. Where's Sophie?"

"I don't know," said Sharon. "She was in the kitchen."

Larry Kirk went down to Sophie's bed and pulled out an old pink rug. He went to the side door and tossed the rug into the driveway. It was folded over when it landed. He stared at it for a while, then he went outside and straightened it.

A moment later, he was back upstairs in bed. The lights were out.

"So when Rags starts to growl," said the radio host, "it means he wants to go for a ride. Is that right?"

"Unless he's already in a car," said the caller. "Then it means he wants to get out and get some exercise."

Larry Kirk blinked. "I can't sleep when people are talking," he said.

"Don't worry," said Sharon. "This show's almost over."

"I hope so," he said. "I'm tired."

"I want to thank you for calling, sir," said the radio host. "It's been interesting. And scientific."

"It's science, all right," said the caller. "But that's not the point. The point is, very few people are willing to pay money to find out what's going on in their pets' heads. My real living," he said, "I make as a cook."

"Really?" said the host. "That surprises me."

Ten minutes later, Larry Kirk was dreaming. He and Sharon were in a restaurant, and a waiter was carrying a plant to their table. Once it was placed in front of him, Larry Kirk could see that it wasn't a plant at all but a moose's head. Leaves growing on the antlers gave it the appearance of a plant, but from his experience, it was doing something that plants don't do: it was barking.

Larry Kirk sat up in bed. The dog was back. He moved Sharon's hand off his stomach and went over to the window. The dog was sitting on the pink rug in the driveway. Larry Kirk opened the window and stuck his head out. He pointed a finger down at the dog.

"Stay," he said.

Paul Hoffman was sitting forward on his couch, chewing a piece of gum and leafing through an old magazine. On one of the pages was a puzzle—a drawing of a carnival with little pictures of objects you had to try to find. Paul Hoffman found the umbrella and the bow tie. He saw something that looked like a marshmallow, but that wasn't on the list. He was searching for the airplane when the phone rang.

It was Larry Kirk. "Am I speaking to Paul Howard?" he asked.

"Hoffman," said Paul Hoffman. "Paul Hoffman."

"All right," said Larry Kirk. "Listen, this is the guy who has your dog."

"I know," said Paul Hoffman.

"Okay," said Larry Kirk. "Good. Now you hung up on me, then you said you were coming to get him. I didn't believe you, but you still said it, and if you're getting sick of this, well, so am I, but the fact is, you never came and nothing ever happened. I just called to tell you that I'm going to make it easy for you."

"What are you talking about?" said Paul Hoffman.

"It's simple," said Larry Kirk. "This is the deal: I got the dog in my driveway right now, and another guy is on his way over. When he gets here, we're going to catch your dog in a big net, drive over to your house, and throw him through your picture window. Because that seems to be about the only way you'll pay any attention to what I'm telling you."

Paul Hoffman listened. The back of his neck was itchy, but both his hands were on the telephone. "I still don't understand," he said quietly, "what makes you think that it's my dog."

Larry Kirk exhaled loudly. "I think it's your dog," he said, "because it has a collar with a tag, and on the tag it says your name. So I called Information, and she gave me your number, and I called you up, and you answered. You can deny whatever you want to, but the fact is, you answered the telephone, and that's how I know he is your dog."

Paul Hoffman's jaw was tired from chewing. "I used to have a dog," he said. "Until about three years ago. But it was small and brown—a cocker spaniel." He found a Styrofoam cup with orange juice in the bottom. He dropped his gum into it.

"Maybe you never got a good look at it," said Larry Kirk. "Because now it's big and black. Might be part Labrador. I don't know."

"It's not the same one," said Paul Hoffman. "Our dog isn't around anymore. He got into a bad fight with one of the dogs in the next block. I had to have him put to sleep." Paul Hoffman thought about the little dog they used to have. He pictured the pink spots at the corners of its eyes.

"What did the tag look like?" asked Larry Kirk.

"It was gold," said Paul Hoffman. "And it was shaped like an octagon, or maybe a hexagon. I'm not sure."

"Come and get your dog, then," said Larry Kirk. "Come and get your dog. Because that's what this one's wearing. Mike's on his way over, so if you don't get here pretty fast, I'm afraid your dog might come sailing into your living room."

"But I still have that tag," said Paul Hoffman.

"I don't think you do," said Larry Kirk. "I don't see how you could. In fact—uh-oh, I think I hear Mike. Yeah, that's what I thought—here comes Mike, pulling into my driveway."

Paul Hoffman heard Larry Kirk hang up, but he held the receiver to his ear for a moment. He wished he did have a lost dog so he could bring it back home and put everything back in order. It would be simple. He could say "Bad dog" or "Bad Spot" or "How could you do a thing like this?" He would have his hand on the dog's collar. He would want his face to seem threatening, but it wouldn't matter. The dog would know the difference.

Paul Hoffman's window was open, but he couldn't hear anything outside. He didn't really believe the guy on the phone would throw a dog into his house. But what would he do? Paul Hoffman wondered how the guy got in touch with him in the first place. There were no dog tags around with his address on them. Unless Cathy had used the old tag on a new dog. Then it was her house the guy was talking about. But she would never do that. Or would she? What other possibilities were there?

Something was yellow, according to the guy, and some numbers were nailed to a tree. Paul Hoffman put down the phone and reached over to close the window. A light came on in a house across the street. It was almost 2:00 A.M., but some part of him expected everyone to suddenly wake up. He was at the point where anything seemed possible. A large moth flew toward him, but at the last second it bounced off the screen. Paul Hoffman flinched. He closed the window.

He had to go and get this dog.

The street Paul Hoffman was looking for began with a B. He'd seen one called Belmont, and one called Burke Avenue, but neither of those had sounded right. He stopped in front of an all-night convenience store. He realized he didn't know what to ask, but the store was right there. That had to count for something.

A man with a thin black mustache and an apron was standing behind the counter. He looked up. Paul Hoffman almost said good night to him, but then he remembered that good night meant goodbye no matter what time of day it was.

"How're you doing?" Paul Hoffman said.

"Not bad," said the cashier. "How about you?"

"I'm okay," said Paul Hoffman. He didn't need to buy anything, but he didn't want to make the cashier nervous, so he started down one of the aisles. He came back to the register holding a bag of cashews, a coloring book, and a tiny container of mint ice cream. He set each item on the counter.

"Four eighty-one," said the cashier. "What you got, a sick kid?"

Paul Hoffman took out his wallet and handed the cashier five dollars. "Yeah," he said. He looked at some magazine covers while the cashier figured his change. One of the covers showed a woman skiing in a bathing suit.

"What's wrong with him?" asked the cashier. "Or is it a her?"

Paul Hoffman held out his hand for the change. "It's a

him," he said. "And he's okay. He's just feeling a little sad. All he has is a little stomachache."

"Sure you don't want a bottle of ginger ale, or something?"

Paul Hoffman was still looking at the magazine rack. On one of the other covers, two rhinoceroses were lying on a rock. "No, thanks," he said. "The ice cream will settle him."

Next to the rhinoceroses was a real-estate magazine. It was laid out in newsprint. The cover was outlined in light blue and featured snapshots of houses. Some of the pictures showed the entire lot, some just showed the front of the house. Paul Hoffman saw that the magazine was free, and he picked up a copy. He tried to see if any people were standing in their yards. But then he realized there couldn't be anyone in the pictures, or the houses would never get sold. The houses had to seem empty. No one wants to feel like an intruder.

"Tell you what, though," said the cashier. "I wouldn't give him any of those nuts."

"No," said Paul Hoffman. "The nuts are for me."

Larry Kirk was sitting on the steps by the side of his house. The dog was twenty feet in front of him, chewing on the rug. Larry Kirk would chase the dog away, but it would come back five minutes later. This had been going on since he'd called Paul Hoffman. Mike hadn't shown up. At first, Larry had tried to be quiet. It was the middle of the night, and everyone else in the neighborhood was probably sleeping. But after a while, he didn't care what happened, and he'd started to yell at the dog. The dog would run faster when Larry Kirk yelled, and looked back at him less often, but it still kept coming back. Now Larry Kirk was just sitting on his porch steps, wondering if it was worth it to get body work done on his car. He was trying not to think about the dog.

Paul Hoffman tossed the realty magazine on his dashboard. He was sliding it down so it wouldn't block his defogger, when he remembered what it was that was supposed to be yellow: a real-estate office. The one on Shennelton. In fact, that was the guy's street, the one off Shennelton, at the light, and even if Paul Hoffman didn't know the house numbers, he knew where they could be found: on a tree. He reached into his bag and pulled out the ice cream. The outside of the container was wet. He lifted the top, and inside was green ice cream with small brown flecks—chocolate chips. He raised the container to his mouth and licked. He sat there for a moment. The ice cream tasted good, but he suddenly had the sensation it didn't belong to him. He closed the container and looked around. Then he put the ice cream back under the seat and started the car.

"I don't understand," said Larry Kirk, "why some people keep dogs like that. On purpose, I mean." He turned the light on.

Sharon covered her eyes. "What?" she said.

"Dogs like that," he said. "People must want them around." He sat on the bed and took off one of his socks. "They must like them."

Sharon squinted. "What about Sophie?" she asked. "What's the difference?"

"This doesn't have anything to do with Sophie," said Larry Kirk. "The difference is, Sophie's a good companion. You can play with her. When you come home, she comes over and licks your face. No matter what. But that dog," he said, gesturing toward the side of the house, "that dog is of no use to anyone. I can't imagine anybody expecting anything from that dog." He pulled off his other sock.

"Were you really going to try and catch it?" asked Sharon.

"If Mike ever showed up with the net," said Larry Kirk. "Good old Mike. I give him five bucks, then I lure the dog over. I think it was finally getting it into its head to leave, but I go ahead and lure it back for the sake of the plan. So Mike decides to stay in bed, and now I've got the damn dog for good." He imagined himself carrying the dog over his shoulder and dropping it at the feet of someone who was supposed to be Paul Hoffman. The dog had X's instead of eyes.

"When you think about it," he said, "it makes sense that a guy who would choose a dog like that for his family would be embarrassed to admit it."

"Maybe he's telling the truth," said Sharon.

"His name is on the tag," said Larry Kirk. "What else do you need?"

Sharon rested her chin on her hands. "There're people who do that for a living," she said. "Capture dogs, I mean."

"I know that," said Larry Kirk. "But the thing is, the people who do that for a living are exactly the kind of people who have no business wandering around in my yard. I'm sorry. I knew some kids like that when I was growing up."

Sharon put her head back down on the pillow.

"You know what I mean," he said. "The kind of kids that knew how to take apart a washing machine motor in high school and always talked big, but the very next time you see them, ten years later or whatever, they're hanging out in your driveway, snooping around and carrying a little bag with whatever it is they use inside it. Dog whistles. Dart guns. I don't know. All I'm saying is, 'No, thanks.'"

"I put an ad in the paper," said Sharon.

"An ad?"

Sharon nodded. "For the dog," she said. "They're supposed to run it tomorrow morning."

"That's not going to do any good," said Larry Kirk. He got in bed and turned out the light. "That's a waste of money," he said. He could hear the dog's toenails clicking around on the pavement below. "How much did it cost?"

"Six dollars a day," said Sharon. "For three days."

The clicking stopped. Larry Kirk sat up. "What is that?" he asked. "Is that a car?"

. . .

The first thing Paul Hoffman noticed about the street had to do with the trees: they all had numbers nailed to them. He listened for a dog barking, hoping he could find the place that way. After about half a block, he came to a stop sign. As the car slowed, he thought he heard someone calling. Then he was certain.

"Hey!" said the voice. "Hold on!"

Paul Hoffman turned to his right. A man wearing a large red sweatshirt and a baseball cap looked in from the passenger window. He was carrying a flashlight that had heavy duct tape wrapped around it. His sleeves were rolled up, and his arms were hanging into the car.

"You looking for something?" asked the man.

Paul Hoffman stared at the duct tape. It was silver. "I'm looking for a dog," he said.

The man nodded. "I'm supposed to be cutting the grass," he said. He turned his head to the side and spat.

Paul Hoffman looked at the man.

"Listen," said the man, "it wasn't my idea." He scratched his chin with the flashlight. "I was supposed to cut it for the past two weeks, but I never got around to it, so now I'm not allowed in the house until it's done. Simple. I call it going along with whatever you have to, to keep everybody happy. No big deal. So anyway, I'll tell you what: you take me to get a pack of cigarettes, and I'll help you find your dog. How's that sound?"

"I don't want to waste a lot of time," said Paul Hoffman. "And I really don't have that much to go on."

"Sure you do," said the man. "What's he look like?"

"I'm not sure," said Paul Hoffman. "I think it's black. Black and white."

"Okay," said the man. "Is he a big dog?"

"He seems big," said Paul Hoffman. "He seems like a pretty good-sized dog."

"What's his name? Maybe we can yell out his name a few times and he'll come to us."

Paul Hoffman picked a thread off his sleeve. "I don't know," he said.

The man blinked. "You had this dog a long time?" he asked. "I'm not trying to be rude or anything, but I think you're lucky you didn't lose your damn dog a long time ago." He laughed.

Paul Hoffman grinned. He made a gesture with his hands that meant he didn't understand it, either. He didn't feel like trying to explain.

"Let's get the cigarettes," said the man. "We'll find your dog in a little while. First my smokes, then your pooch. How about it?" He slapped his free hand against the inside of the car door.

"I guess so," said Paul Hoffman. He didn't know where the dog was, anyway. The man opened the door and got inside. Paul Hoffman made a slow U-turn and headed back toward the convenience store. First the smokes, then the pooch.

"I appreciate this," said the man. His flashlight was on the seat. He noticed Paul Hoffman looking at it. "I'm supposed to tape it to my wrist," he said. "So I can see what I'm doing." He placed the flashlight alongside his wrist so Paul Hoffman could see what he meant. "My wife thought of it," he said. "I had to admit it was a good idea. I can't very well hold it in my hand."

"No," said Paul Hoffman. "I don't see how you could."

Inside the store, the man walked straight to the counter.

"Let me have two packs of Salems," he said. "And some matches."

The cashier looked at Paul Hoffman, then turned to get the cigarettes. There was a large container of pretzel rods next to the cash register. Paul Hoffman hadn't noticed it the first time he was there. He felt around in his pocket for some change. He found nineteen cents.

"I'll take one of those," he said, pointing to the pretzels.

The cashier reached into the jar. "How's your boy feeling?" he asked.

Paul Hoffman coughed. "Oh, he's doing fine," he said. "Much better. What do I owe you?"

"Three cents," said the cashier. "And you," he said to the man, "two dollars and thirty-eight." He set the cigarettes on the counter.

"Put them together," said the man. He gave the cashier a ten-dollar bill.

The cashier handed Paul Hoffman the pretzel. "He have any trouble keeping that ice cream down?" he asked.

"Nope," said Paul Hoffman. "No trouble. He put it away like a champ."

"That's probably what made him come around, then," said the cashier, giving the man his change. "A lot of times, that's all it takes."

"I think you're right," said Paul Hoffman. He put the pretzel into his shirt pocket. "Okay, then," he said.

"All right," said the cashier. "You gentlemen have a good evening."

Back in the car, Paul Hoffman took a bite of his pretzel.

"You got a kid, huh?" said the man, lighting a cigarette. "Bet he misses his dog."

"He probably does," said Paul Hoffman. "I don't know." He was waiting at the light near the real-estate place.

"Kids never understand things like that," said the man. "I bet he thinks it's your fault the dog is gone. I bet that's why you're out here right now."

"Because it's my fault?" Paul Hoffman asked. He turned to the man.

"Because the kid thinks it's your fault," said the man.

"It's got nothing to do with me," said Paul Hoffman. He changed his grip on the steering wheel. "It was her. Not me." He watched his pretzel vibrate. It was moving with the rhythm of the engine.

"Her?" said the man. "You mean your wife?"

"It's her dog," said Paul Hoffman. "I don't even live there anymore. I don't even know what I'm doing out here." The light changed. He turned left.

"So how are you going to find it?" asked the man.

"I don't know," said Paul Hoffman. "That's what I was trying to tell you. I guess I was hoping I would hear it somehow. A guy from this neighborhood called me. Larry somebody. He said it was hanging around his yard. He said it was up to me to take care of it. At first I thought he was crazy, but now I'm starting to think he's right."

"Larry, huh?" said the man. "Let me see. Larry." He flicked some ashes into the ashtray. "What are you going to do if you find it?"

"I don't know," said Paul Hoffman. "She said she didn't want to see me, or hear from me. No visits, no phone calls, no letters." He noticed the radio was on, but with the volume all the way down. He turned it off. "I don't know what you're supposed to say to that. So I said okay."

"What else can you say when things go that far?" said the man. He shook his head. "I'll tell you what you can say. You can't say a damn thing."

Paul Hoffman shrugged. "Anyway," he said, "I'm pretty sure this is the guy's street."

"Could very well be," said the man. Then he put both his hands on the dashboard and looked back over his shoulder. "Whoa," he said. "You just passed my house."

Paul Hoffman stopped the car. "Sorry," he said. "Let me back up."

"Don't worry about it," said the man. "This is perfect." He got out, then leaned back in and grabbed his flashlight.

"Thanks," he said, closing the door.

"It's okay," said Paul Hoffman. "Thanks for the pretzel."

"No problem," said the man. "Listen, if I hear anything strange, like a dog or whatever, I'll look for you. All right? All right." He tapped his fingers on the top of the car.

Paul Hoffman watched the man walk at an angle up the lawn. Then he put the car in gear and rolled slowly past the next few houses.

He imagined Cathy asleep in their bed. In the back yard there was a small circular area where the grass had stopped growing. At the center of the circle was a doghouse. Attached to the side of the doghouse was a chain. The chain was broken.

Paul Hoffman's head jerked forward. He opened his eyes. Something was moving toward the street in front of him. He hit his brake and the car went into a slight skid. When the car was no longer moving, he let out his breath. A dog was running through the beams from his headlights. It stopped in the street and looked at Paul Hoffman. Its eyes reflected. Then it turned away and took off along a hedgerow. Paul Hoffman stared after the dog until it disappeared between two houses.

"What did you stop for?" said a voice.

Paul Hoffman turned and saw a man in a gray T-shirt and jeans standing by the edge of the road. The man was breathing hard, and his hair was sticking up. He was holding one end of an old pink rug.

"You wouldn't have had to kill him," said the man. "You could've just run over his foot or something. It doesn't kill them. It just makes them . . . all disoriented." He lifted his hands and waved them back down. "Now he'll come right back again."

Paul Hoffman noticed a tree near the house behind the man. There were numbers on the tree—a 1, a 7, and a 1.

"Larry?" he said.

The man moved closer to Paul Hoffman. "Who are you?" he said. He tried to see inside the car.

"Paul Hoffman."

Larry Kirk's eyes widened. "You," he said. "Jesus. You almost ran over your own dog."

Paul Hoffman shivered. He noticed the dog creeping back toward them. He got out of his car. The engine was still running.

"Watch," said Larry Kirk. "Here he comes again."

Paul Hoffman looked at Larry Kirk, then at the dog. It was in the middle of the street.

Paul Hoffman knelt down. He heard a siren. It made him wonder if maybe Larry had been disturbing the peace. But after a few seconds the sound died away.

"I came to look at the tag," said Paul Hoffman. "I never saw this dog before."

The dog seemed wary of him, but it came closer. It sniffed. Paul Hoffman wondered if the dog could possibly recognize his smell. It'd been six months since he'd been in that house. He snapped his fingers. The dog's ears perked up. There was something about this dog of Cathy's Paul Hoffman felt he understood. He looked at the dog's face. Maybe they were where they were for the same reasons. Then he thought of Larry's dog, Sophie.

"He knows you," said Larry Kirk. "What did you do, hit your head on something? It's your own damn dog!"

Paul Hoffman rubbed his hands on his pant legs. The dog approached him, this time even more carefully. Finally he could see the tag. It was six-sided and said:

P. HOFFMAN
16 W. HOWARD

"Now will you take him home?" said Larry Kirk.

Paul Hoffman stood up. He was thinking about what it said on the tag. He looked back at his car and thought of the apartment where he was living. He slid his hand under the dog's collar. The dog stiffened, then relaxed. "Come on," said Paul Hoffman. "Let's go."

"Where is that, anyway?" asked Larry Kirk. "West Howard."

"South side," said Paul Hoffman. He opened the car door. The dog jumped in back.

"Your dog came a long way, then."

"I know," said Paul Hoffman. He got into the car.

"And you got a long drive ahead of you. Twenty-five minutes, at least."

"It's not that far," said Paul Hoffman. "Maybe fifteen." He adjusted his mirror. "Doesn't even matter. I'm only going as far as the Highlander apartments."

"The Highlander?"

"Yeah," said Paul Hoffman. He rolled his window halfway up and looked at Larry Kirk. "That's where I'm staying now."

Larry Kirk shook his head.

"It's a long story," said Paul Hoffman.

Larry Kirk took a step back from the car. "Do me a favor," he said. "I don't want to hear it."

The dog was sitting up on the backseat. When Paul Hoffman looked into the rearview mirror, he saw the dog staring at him. Except for its small white eyebrows, the dog's face was black. Paul Hoffman turned around as often as he could, but when he tried to touch the dog, it moved out of his reach. It slid across the seat and put its head out the window. After Paul Hoffman turned to face forward, it started chewing on the armrest.

Paul Hoffman was taking the dog to his apartment. That was as far as he could go for the moment.

Paul Hoffman found a piece of rope and tied the dog to the handle on the refrigerator door. Then he went into the bathroom. He looked at himself in the mirror as he washed his face. He needed to sleep.

When he returned to the kitchen, the dog was lying on the floor eating a piece of pizza.

"No," said Paul Hoffman. "Bad."

The dog didn't look up.

Paul Hoffman undid the rope and tied it to a table leg across the room. He put some newspaper down around the dog. He got a small bowl and filled it with water. It was Cathy's bowl. Tomorrow he'd talk to her. He'd have to. He set the bowl in front of the dog.

"Here," he said. "Have some water. I'm going to bed."

Paul Hoffman woke up to a curious noise. It sounded to him like a rusty wheel being forced to turn, or the cry of a large bird—a chicken, or maybe a turkey. He wasn't fully awake, and he didn't want to move right away. It seemed important to him to try to remember if he'd ever actually seen a live turkey. If not, how could he know what one really sounded like? He waited until he heard the sound again, then he looked at his clock. It was only 7:15. He got out of bed and walked to the kitchen. That's where the sound seemed to be coming from. The sun was up, but Paul Hoffman could tell the day was going to be cloudy. He stood in the kitchen doorway.

The dog was lying asleep on the floor, next to the newspapers Paul Hoffman had laid out. Its mouth was closed, but the dog was making the strange noise. Paul Hoffman took a step closer. He realized what was happening: the dog was barking in its sleep. Its legs twitched, and the yelping became more troubled. Paul Hoffman tried to imagine what was going on in the dog's dream. He wondered if Larry was chasing the dog, or if the dog was riding in the back of his car. Then he thought of something else. Maybe the dog was dreaming of moving from one strange place to another, and never getting home.

Paul Hoffman made a move to wake the dog, but stopped himself. He stood still. He stood so still he could hear his own breathing in between the dog's muffled barks.

Paul Hoffman slept until three o'clock that afternoon. It was Sunday. He felt he could have slept longer, but someone rang his doorbell. He told the person to wait downstairs until he was dressed. He didn't want anyone to know he had a dog in his apartment.

When Paul Hoffman got to the lobby, a young woman was

sitting in a chair reading a brochure. She looked up when he got near her. She was wearing sandals and orange shorts, and her hair was wet. She'd been standing in the rain.

"Mr. Hoffman?" she said.

Paul Hoffman scratched his arm. "Yes," he said. "Paul Hoffman. Hi."

"Hi," said the woman. "I got your name from Sharon Kirk."

"Sharon Kirk," he said. "I'm not sure I know who that is."

The woman laughed. "There's been a lot of confusion," she said. "I knew I never should have used that tag."

"I don't understand," said Paul Hoffman.

"It looked so legal," she said. "And it was only going to be temporary. I didn't have time to get one of my own, a real one, so I just used the one from the box. I bought this box of junk at a garage sale—some earrings and some medals—it seemed like a good deal for a dollar. But there was also this dog tag, and I wasn't planning on getting a dog or anything, but the next thing I knew, a friend of Jerry's was moving and he couldn't take Riley with him. I couldn't help myself. I just stuck the tag on him. You know, temporarily, so he wouldn't get picked up. But I never meant to cause so much trouble." She laughed again, then she shook her head. "Anyway," she said, "I saw Sharon's ad in the newspaper and I called her. She sent me here. So here I am."

Paul Hoffman noticed he'd been staring at the woman's arm.

"Believe me, I never meant to tell you all this," she said. "I feel like a real jerk." She'd folded the brochure in half and was running her fingers along the crease.

Paul Hoffman was replaying certain parts of her explanation. What was she trying to tell him? He looked past her through the glass security door out into the street. The rain was steady, but it still seemed to Paul Hoffman like a good day for a drive.

"So where do I fit in?" he asked, trying to smile.

The woman looked at him. "Well," she said, "I guess you're the one who goes upstairs and gets me my dog. Or outside, or around back, or wherever he is."

"I'm not sure I know what you're talking about," said Paul Hoffman.

He touched the doorknob.

"I do not have a dog." **Q**

What Makes You Think You Deserve This?

He had come to them to ask for money. They were his mother's friends. He didn't know them very well, and hadn't known that they would be so old. They were immeasurably old, the man and the woman, preserved by their immense wealth, like butterflies in a glass case. That was not something he had remembered about them. But then he didn't have a good memory for faces. He had always thought of himself as someone who cared about people. But no. It was true. He simply cut them off. All his life he had discarded friends like yesterday's newspapers. "See you soon," he'd say, then never see them again.

Still, they were cordial enough. They seemed to know what he had come for. The man, the husband, was seated in a chair. He lifted one arm high into the air and waved, as if he were on a boat pulling away from the dock. She met him at the door. "Oh, we were just talking about you," she said.

"Nothing bad, I hope," he replied, proud, under the circumstances, that he could muster any trace of wit.

"What was that?" She thumped the side of her head, as if to shake something loose.

He spoke louder. "Nothing bad, I hope."

"I'm sorry?"

"I said, *Nothing bad,* I hope."

"Please forgive me." She was smiling. Her head was tilted expectantly.

"It doesn't matter."

"I'm afraid you'll have to speak up. My aid's on the fritz." She thumped the side of her head once again.

"I said, *It doesn't matter.*"

Her smile faded. She looked at him curiously, her head still tilted for a very long time.

He was surprised at how many people they had working in their home. The hallway was crowded with men and women in dark business suits. Youngish men and women. In their mid-forties. At the heights of their careers. They smiled and nodded as they passed the old woman, but she appeared not to notice. "We've heard so much about you," she was saying.

"Nothing bad, I hope." How could he have said that again? And how was he going to ask for money with all these people around? He had to get a grip on himself.

"Oh no, no. We're surrounded by your admirers."

Now he was in the bathroom. He'd walked in the door and practically the first thing he'd said was, "Where's your bathroom?" That was a mistake. That was definitely not the way to handle these venerable people. He looked at himself in the mirror: a rumpled man in his mid-forties. Stains on his dove-gray shirt, no tie, the embarrassment of his pink dome concealed only by a mat of lacquered strands brushed over from his temple. In his hands he held his penis, which was surprisingly long, brown, and of no particular shape.

"I just want you to know," said the man, "that we've signed all the papers. It's all taken care of. So you have nothing to worry about."

He, the younger man, the supplicant, felt momentarily grateful. But something was wrong. He had forgotten something. He couldn't quite think of what.

"Let's drink to your success," said the man, who was lying on his back, on an antique invalid's couch made of iron bars and varnished oak, with big white baby-carriage wheels. He was holding a glass straight up in the air, and the younger man didn't see how he was going to be able to drink from it without spilling what was in it all over his face.

The woman came up to the younger man with a sweaty glass of clear liquid. He took it greedily. He was very thirsty.

"We love you very much," she said, giving his hand a squeeze.

"I love you, too," he said, blushing deeply. She knew he was lying.

"I hear you've come to ask for money," said the cook, a sturdy pink woman with the solid buttocks of a farm animal and skin as smooth as a baby's. Her voice was dull, as if she were talking in her sleep, except it had a cruelish inflection.

"I've already got it," he said proudly.

"No, you don't." She didn't look around. She was cutting chunks of raw beef. "Have they told you when you're going to get it?"

"No," he answered. This is what he had forgotten to ask.

"Have they told you how much?"

"No." He had forgotten to ask this as well. Money talk always embarrassed him.

He didn't understand the next thing she said, something about how they couldn't be trusted. Then she said, "It all depends on me." She still wasn't looking at him. Her voice was still dull and cruel. But he realized that she wanted him to come into her.

After that there was some confusion. The cook was lying facedown on the wet, concrete kitchen floor. He was in her, very close to orgasm, but something was not right. "No, that's not it," she said. And then the old woman was standing in the doorway with her hands on her hips. "Look." She pointed with a gnarled finger. He looked where the old woman was pointing and saw that the seam between the cook's buttocks was smooth and pink and completely without blemish. But that was irrelevant. He was so close to an orgasm. He wanted the old woman to go away. She grabbed his wrist with her bony hand and said, "Come with me."

The old man was sitting in a chair now, at a huge table. He raised his glass and said in a hearty voice, "Hail the master of the house and manor." The younger man was touched by how completely this couple had taken him in. There were tears in his eyes. But he couldn't pay attention to what they were saying. The cook was crouched under the table, between his legs, performing fellatio, although neither of the old people seemed to notice. A vast meal had been laid out in front of him: buckets of soup, fish with their heads on, pineapples, coconuts, and something long and pink that twitched as if it were still alive. The old couple had not even lifted a crumb onto their plates, but the younger man had already had three helpings. "Eat! Eat!" they said. "You're still a growing boy." He wanted to say something about how he was no longer growing, but his mouth was packed tight and he was lost in the cook's warm, long throat. He kept spilling things all over the floor, big things: chicken legs, doughnuts, tomatoes. They made loud noises as they fell, but no one seemed to notice. He just hoped they wouldn't bend over and see.

The old woman was leading him by the wrist through the basement of her home. It was very dark. The floors were littered with garbage, gravel, broken glass. Oozing black beards of bacteria hung down the walls and water gathered in puddles on the floor, running in rills amid the garbage. All around them, mostly obscured by darkness, loomed the great flanks of machines, badly rusted, lumpy with the same oozing growth as the walls. After a while, he began to suspect that he was actually walking through his own guts, but she explained that they were inside a ship that had spent many years submerged beneath the North Atlantic. "That's why it's all such a mess," she said. Now that she'd mentioned it, he could see the long rusty drive shaft that was connected to the ship's propeller. At one point, they had to slide under the shaft and over the top of a wide machine. The space was very narrow and they had to lie flat on their backs. Cold water soaked up through their clothing, gravel dug into their spines. But it wasn't too bad, really. When he had finally lowered himself to the floor on the other side of the machine, he saw that the old woman was already halfway up a slimy and badly corroded ladder. He followed her up into the open air.

"All of this will be yours," she was saying. They were on a very high hill, perhaps a mountain, and could see for hundreds of miles in all directions to the point where the blue of the earth blended into the blue of the sky. The sun was out. A strong wind was whipping their hair and the grass at their feet. He watched as tall clouds drifted toward them, pushing blue shadows over the rising and falling green of the land. "Enjoy it!" she said. She had to shout because of the wind. "You don't have to be ashamed. You're rich now! It's a wonderful thing!" Directly in front of them, along the edge of a lake, was a city that looked like a heap of cigarette ash on a lush carpet of moss. In the middle of the city there was a huge white building in the shape of a woman's leg. It was still under construction. Tiny people were crawling all over it like ants. They were dangling from threads that were swept into graceful arcs by the wind. On the far side of the city there was a mountain tall enough to be powdered with snow. And beyond that: the blue earth and the blue sky.

"How long until all of this is mine?" he asked.

"What was that?" she said, thumping the side of her head.

"I'm sorry," she said.

"Please forgive me," she said.

He shouted into the wind. **Q**

Screaming

I thought she had grabbed her whole pearl necklace in a fist to stop it at her throat so that we could speak, because it had been crashing into itself, back and forth across her breast, as she was moving toward me.

"Your dog Heather"—was all I could think to say to her—"I still remember your story about Heather, your dog, and about your daughter coming down the stairs in the black wig."

"That was Heidi," she said.

"Your daughter is Heidi?"

"No," she said, "that's the dog."

"Oh, and she's not living," I said as she let the pearls go and they fell back down against her chest.

"That's right," she said. "Heather is. Heather's a better name—that's why you remember Heather. Heather is—" and she rolled her eyes so that I would know that I should have remembered Heather.

We did not talk about Heidi anymore that night, and I did not bring her up for conversation, because I did not have to. I spoke to her husband instead.

Still, I remembered how when the daughter was coming down the stairs in the black wig, wearing the kimono, Heidi ran away. I want to say that Heidi ran away screaming when she saw the daughter—but Heidi is the dog. She was a dog.

For the sake of conversation, when her husband and I saw a woman neither of us knew, I said, "I bet she's not afraid of a living soul." I said it because the woman had obviously done her hair all by herself for this gala—just stuck bobby pins you could see into her white hair, just worn an old, out-of-fashion cotton dress.

I told the husband I'd like to shake that woman's hand and ask her if it was true what I had guessed.

I was considering it, getting up close. I wondered would she get scared or what she would do—what I would do.

"What about that one there?" her husband asked.

That one there was a woman who was trying to get back behind my husband. The woman was wincing as if she had just done something awful.

"A gambling problem—that's what she has," I said. But that wasn't sordid enough. So then I said, "I don't have a clue."

"Now me," the husband said. "Do me."

"You," I said, "you are hardworking. You are—"

"No," he said, *"not that—"* The man looked frightened. He looked ready to hear what I would say as if I really knew.

Then someone was at my back, tugging at my hair, moving it. I felt a mouth was on the nape of my neck. It was a kiss.

I did not have the faintest idea who would want to do that to me. There was not a soul.

When I saw him, when I turned, his head was still hung down low from kissing me. He was full of shame.

Thank God that I did not know who he was.

I kept my face near his. I liked the look of him.

I was praying he would do something more to me. Anything. **Q**

Public Works

It doesn't make any difference when you know about the Swiss Alps, when you know that they were actually a public-works project—probably the largest in history. They're still impressive. Maybe even more so. It explains the tunnels, too, which *I've* always been impressed by. I can't really explain why. She can, though. And has. Don't ever travel in a car with someone who has read *Psychopathia Sexualis* and done her doctoral work on Krafft-Ebing. I didn't buy it, anyway. I think it's just the engineering, something about the smoothness, the uniformity, the aseptic quality to it, something about the amount of precision it took—even if they did build the mountains on top of the tunnels instead of carving one from the other.

People always talk about the Alps as the heart of Swiss foreign policy. Right enough. The Swiss aren't even part of the UN, for God's sake! They have a "citizens army"; everyone has a submachine gun at home in his closet. Well, maybe not everyone. The Swiss didn't give women the vote until the early seventies. I don't know what the typical lag-time is between getting the franchise and getting automatic weapons. I can't really see that system working in New York. Or I can, and it's too vivid. Anyway, foreign policy or not, the Alps were definitely the beginning of genuine Swiss prosperity. Skiing is a piece of it, of course. But there's a lot more. In large part, it was a demonstration of Swiss ingenuity and perseverance. And, finally, it got Switzerland out of the Depression, between the wars, and kept it genuinely safe during the Second World War.

She got tired of the Alps thing real quick, not two days after we left Geneva, when we were still in Grindelwald, trying to decide whether it was worth eighty dollars in rides to get to the top of the Jungfrau. I thought it was. And I liked the idea. She didn't speak German, didn't know why I thought it was funny. Or I didn't think she did, anyway.

"Your sexuality is determined when you're a child," she said, "by who took your temperature when you were sick, and how."

"Well, my neighbor took my temperature," I said, trying to make it as neutral as possible. "And she was a nurse, and she did it by putting the thermometer in my armpit."

She raised an eyebrow at this.

"Didn't Krafft-Ebing approve of axillary temperature-taking?"

"No, he went in for basal body temperature," she shot back.

Basal body temperature. She didn't believe in birth control. But she didn't believe in pregnancy, either. And she was completely without rhythm—in that sense, anyway. She had a thermometer which only registered a couple of degrees, between 98 and 100, Fahrenheit, big notches for tenths of degrees, very sensitive. She took her temperature every morning before getting out of bed, kept a chart of this in her journal, knew when she was ovulating. So she said. But she was a diabetic and her metabolism wasn't to be trusted. A powerful aphrodisiac, uncertainty.

Some parts of traveling together we had worked out perfectly: border drills. We took off our sunglasses, I took out my earring. We smiled and looked married, even if the passports said different. No foreign languages at borders, no kidding, no mistakes. English, smiles, and cooperation. When the ferry landed in East Germany, at Warnemünde, they X-rayed my toothpaste; my teeth glittered like new for the rest of the summer—but that was with Pete, that was before her, though it was all planned.

It was the same car, when I was with Pete, and it was still

too small: a beautiful red, four-door Golf, with a sunroof and a Blaupunkt stereo. Still too small, no dining car, nowhere to go, no place to retreat to.

"Bother you to be a Jew in Germany?" he asked me.

"Yeah, I don't know, huh? Maybe."

Strange place. Good question. And it was okay until that one day on the Autobahn. An accident—I guess—turned it into a parking lot. We were sunning ourselves on the hood, waiting for it to clear; everyone was. A helicopter—police, green and white with a splash of Day-Glo orange—buzzed low, loudspeaker blasting. I don't know what it said. All I caught was the *"Achtung! Achtung!"* And I know that doesn't mean anything, just "Attention." It's not like *Juden raus!* or anything like that. But it's war-movie stuff, storm troopers and death camps.

The strange part is that I liked Germany, liked it a lot, felt a kinship with it. It's very American; it has to be, it's an occupied country. But beyond that, the highways, the cars, the technology; there's something clean and sharp and hard about Germany that's both attractive and a little frightening.

"Well, at least you know where you're going," Pete said.

"Yeah, Geneva," I said. "The twenty-third."

She had a beautiful body, a beautiful face: chestnut hair, fine, halfway down her back; blue eyes, like Royal Copenhagen porcelain; breasts like pink-tipped tangerines; skin like shaved suede over a perfectly ripe avocado, firm but not hard, no wrinkles, no sags, no bags. I'd always wondered whether a diabetic woman would taste sweet, and she did—briny but sweet, salty but syrupy. And I knew she was cheating high on her blood sugar again, something no one had ever believed me about.

But I had been there last winter, in the emergency room in St. Vincent's. The language of diabetes—harsh—had been tattooed across my mind.

"Why aren't you *complying*?" the nurse had yelled at her. "Why aren't you in *control*?"

Why?

"She always has so much energy," Pete said, as if that was anything other than evidence against her.

"You learn to do what you have to do," she said, deftly shooting into the muscle of her thigh or into her upper arm, only rarely leaving a little half egg of warm, raised skin, when the insulin didn't absorb properly.

"Yeah, well, that's the mechanics of it, not the emotional end."

Not that I could deal with it.

She was ahead of me in everything else. It had been three years and she was definitely the responsible one; she'd finished her doctorate, was ready to become a sex therapist—God help me. I was still working any job I could, working for eight months, saving a thousand dollars at a clip, and going to Europe whether she came with me or not.

"This summer, I'll meet you," she said. "There's a conference in Madrid."

But I wasn't going to Spain, wasn't going to fuck up my Spanish with that ridiculous lisp.

"You come north."

Well, anyway, we knew people in Geneva. It was the summer that Jorge Luis Borges died there; I thought I saw him one day in the park—she told me it was a dream. She had never liked him, anyway. The writing: sure. But he was a reactionary and she couldn't really stomach that. Anyway, dream or not, I spoke to a blind visionary, in the park, in Geneva, and he had an Argentine accent.

"What kind of conference?" Pete asked.

"Fantasies," I told him, as we roared through East Germany, toward Berlin.

"I always wanted to be blown by a bald woman," Pete said. "Head to toes, eyebrows to pubes. While going through a car wash. In a limo. With a sunroof. With my thumb hooked through one of her earrings."

Holy shit, I thought, my best friend has a thing for Mr. Clean.

"I don't even want to begin to tell you what it means," she said.

"I didn't ask you."

There's a church in the middle of West Berlin, half a church, a church and a half. One part of it remains as it must have been at the end of the war, bombed half to rubble. The new part is modernistic, like a honeycomb. I guess they're trying to prove that they're contrite, that they want to remember, that they know they were bad. But somehow it only says the opposite to me, that we're bad. It's an occupied country—both sides—perhaps always will be, if we can still use the word "always."

We were going to go to Prague, Pete and I, but the Czech military attaché in West Berlin was closed on the weekend and we couldn't get visas. Maybe you can get them at the border, maybe you can't, I wasn't going to find out there. We went west instead of south, out Check Point Bravo, to Goslar, a few hours across the border again, camped in rolling hills overlooking a cow pasture, using the car as a windbreak.

The first night in Geneva was strange, as first nights always are. I cherish this. I don't think she fully appreciates the service I do her by our separations. I met her at the main station, as we had planned. She was with a little old Austrian woman who was going somewhere for eye surgery, who was sweet and articulate and senile in four languages, who couldn't see her own feet and was carrying two duffel bags and what looked like a tool box. We got her a hotel room before parting company.

Yves and Brigit moved out of their apartment for us—four blocks east, to Yves's mother's place—leaving only their cat, Olivier, black, with a puff of white at his chest, neurotic and dangerous; he'd scare himself and then blame me. He landed on my shoulder—talons out—the instant I came, and she thought this was just the funniest thing; I usually don't yell.

"It's progress," she soothed.

How I hate that!

"I'm not a patient, present, past, or future."

She speaks Italian and a little French. I speak Russian and a little German. We both speak pretty good Spanish—she's somewhat better. Where we go is a power struggle. In Geneva, she's in control. When we move to Grindelwald, the balance shifts—they speak German there. Travel is about control, as is history: who drives, who interprets, who's on top. And both are unnatural situations, put people in unnatural—frequently unbearable—proximity.

Pete took off for the Loire Valley, for a bike tour of the castles and nuclear reactors of France. We parted friends— only just. You shouldn't travel with anyone you care about.

"Hey, you really blew it with those girls in Stockholm," he said, in parting.

"As if I was interested."

"You were as interested as granite," he said, unstrapping his bike from the top of the Golf. "But, hey, you got something waiting for you."

"Yeah, someone," I said.

"Well, tell her I said . . ."

"He just never grew up," she said, when we'd gotten to northern Yugoslavia, relatively neutral ground, where German was dominant but Italian would get you by. She hadn't liked Hungary, which was cheap but wholly German—if they spoke to you at all.

"And we have?"

"I have, anyway."

She sounded sure, but I knew it was bullshit. Her hair lay curled beside her, like a thick brown snake, on her Garfield the Cat towel, on a cement beach, overlooking the impossibly blue Adriatic. She was topless and beautifully tanned. Only a somewhat pink and swollen area on the top of her left thigh marred the evenness of her tan, head to toes. I touched it lightly, a little half egg of warm, raised skin, where the insulin hadn't absorbed properly.

"So no more hospitals?"

"You going to get a real job?"

Yeah. Maybe.

If the Alps were the greatest public-works project ever; if Switzerland, in the original Helvetian language, indeed does mean "flat land," then Yugoslavia, in Serbo-Croatian, must mean "where we left the rubble," must be either where they quarried the stone for the Swiss Alps or where they dumped the leftovers. It's where we left our rubble, where we promised to comply, on that tacky little resort island in the north, on Krk, just off Rijeka, where the beaches are pebbles or cement, where the Germans and Austrians still reign, where there's even a sporadic American military presence, albeit on R&R. We hammered out the Krk Accord there. And I still don't know what it all means. **Q**

The Light Falling Across It Just So

Way back in the back of the dressing-room closet, back behind the long to-the-floor dresses and behind the spangled-colored sequined dresses, my mama's pink mink cape and hat to match both are tissue-paper-wrapped and stuffed and draped in that kind of plastic they won't let little kids play with, but you can still see the pink glowing through when you turn the closet light on. Someday, when I grow up, that pink mink cape and hat to match are going to be mine.

It's a special-occasion thing, like for a fancy party, with her piled-up blond hair on top of her head, like once when I came in sweaty but cold from outside and saw her and my daddy dressed to go out—her in that pink mink cape and my daddy giving her a long kiss—so long a kiss that the pink mink hat fell off and her hair fell down her back just like in the movies, and I guess they didn't know I was there, because they kept on kissing and kissing each other for such a long time—enough that I figured it would be a good idea for me to just go on back out to play.

Sometimes when my mama is busy with having bridge club at our house, like during the summer, because of our being the ones with air-conditioning, and when my daddy is gone to the office all day—and he hardly ever just drops in—then I go back there into that dressing-room closet, and sometimes I spend the whole afternoon just looking at my mama's and my daddy's things and smelling the powder and the cigarettes and the Shocking by Schiaparelli, as soundless I open and close closets and drawers and look and look and then put back exactly so no one can ever tell I've been in there.

I hang around to watch when the bridge club ladies' day arrives, each one by one saying, "It's so hot!" as she walks in the door and greets my mama with a pretend kiss. First there's a dining-room sit-down lunch with tuna fish and with iced tea. And then, after a silent smoking of cigarettes, and after they carry their chairs into the already-set-up living-room card table, and they talk babies and new houses and how it's somebody's own fault if she's losing her husband—then they sit down and discuss maybe playing for just a little bit of money this time, and they cross their high heels up under their chairs, the nylons wrinkling in clear skin-colored folds around their ankles—all except for Aunt Dorothy, who wears loafers and glasses and keeps score and whose husband was hurt in the war. And then they get down to business.

Lots of times I stay to see Aunt Celeste pick up the cards first—red flashing fingernails shuffling and reshuffling them, her fingers dancers, the cards acrobats who've flown through the air a thousand times. They say she is real smart from some girls' school up East, but I think she doesn't like kids much, and that includes me. She always says to me, "What pretty pink cheeks," and then she sort of glares before she smartly slaps down one card after another card, around and around—four little stacks of cards—her lips moving sideways around her cigarette, the smoke drifting white chiffon across her face.

The cards dealt, the ladies pick them up and raise their four little fans in front of their faces, and Aunt Millie says she isn't good enough to play this hand, and she lays it down and then picks a gardenia out of an arrangement nearby and sticks it in her hair. Then Aunt Celeste says to my mama has she got any bourbon in the house, and that's okay, she'll get it herself, and she gets up while the others are still rearranging their hands.

Once, Aunt Millie made me paper dolls out of newspaper folded again and again while she was playing dummy in the game—and she whispered to me that dummy was her favorite part to play. The paper dolls were strung out, holding newsprint hands, except on the ends, where some were missing arms or legs—a long line of unbroken, attached-together dolls with hair and dresses just alike, and she drew little faces on them, smiling all their lips in Crayola.

In my room I thumbtacked them up, circle-eyed grinning faces all the same, newsprint headlines running across their bodies and their just-alike dresses and their sometimes-missing arms and legs, and my daddy came and sang me a bedtime song about a man who wanted a paper doll that he could call his own.

The paper dolls I really like to play with are the dime-store cardboard ones my mama bought me, their tall glossy books filled with paper-doll dresses and suits and purses and jewels and things you cut out very carefully, and then you very carefully fold these little paper tabs over the shoulders and around the thin little waists and the tiny little wrists and ankles of the paper dolls. I can't decide whether I like my Myrna Loy paper doll best or my Betty Hutton one, so I play with them both together as if they were friends. The thing about paper dolls is, you can't walk them around or have them doing things all that much, because the clothes and hats and shoes that are attached by just these little folded tabs will all fall away and the paper dolls will be running around in their underpants, like in those dreams where you hope no one will notice, so you have to place the little dresses and jackets and hats and purses and gloves and shoes on them, very carefully folding the tabs perfectly into place, and then when they look just like dream-girl Miss Americas, first you prop them up against something, because they can't stand on their own, and then you have to look at them and look at them and concentrate on how pretty they are and on how lovely and perfect they are, and then you make up the game in your head and pretend to yourself that something is really happening. There are some girls you can play with that will play this with you in just the same way almost—it seems like—forever.

Boys usually won't play this with you for a very long time, but once, this boy who lives next door to me named Nathan and I played with the paper dolls for almost a whole afternoon, on the day when I decided to make pink mink capes and hats to match for both Myrna Loy and Betty Hutton, and also for another paper doll I had then that was a Loretta Young.

It was well into the game on a hot summer bridge-club day, with Aunt Celeste playing the hand in the living room and Nathan and I with the paper dolls all laid out under the dining-room table, and him saying he wanted to quit, because this wasn't real, until I thought of making the paper dolls mink capes and hats to match by cutting up cotton pads and coloring them with watercolors. He said okay, but only if we could go back there in the dressing-room closet and look at the real one first, so we carried all the stuff with us down the hallway past the bridge-club ladies, as though we were going back to my room to play—they weren't noticing us, anyway—and when we got back into the dressing room, we could hear them laughing and talking between hands about who got what and how they'd played it. We could even smell their cigarette smoke when we got back into the closet and were opening my daddy's drawers and looking through his key chains and cuff links and playing cards with naked women on them. He had a lot of stuff like that, and Nathan wanted to take some of it, but I stopped him by starting on my mama's drawers with the stockings and slips and the powder puffs and little red Maybelline boxes with the little gummy brushes in them. We were whispering the whole time, and the smells, dusty-perfumy and dark like the inside of the closet, before I pulled the cord for light and drew aside the dresses to show the glowing plastic-covered pink mink cape and its hat to match that we were going to copy for the paper dolls still in our hands. Then even though I was afraid some-body might come, I untied the cord like I had never done before on top of the plastic bag and pulled it slowly bit by bit down and down, and the pink mink emerging glowing at the top, pale as pale, with softly swaying, alive-like hairs moving in the light, and we stood silent just looking at it, and I could hear Nathan breathing right next to my ear, and then I pulled down the plastic a little more and a little more—and then right in the middle Nathan grabbed up that Loretta Young paper doll, saying he was going to torture her to death, and then he ran through the house with me chasing and the bridge-club ladies exclaiming and my mother getting up to stop us, and he ran out into the yard—paper-doll clothes flying out behind him on all sides and me running and shouting behind, and he threw her into the street right under a car so that she got that hot sticky black tar all over her front side. Then he said, "Oh, she needs a bath," and he threw her into the sprinkler, and then after that she had a wrecked-up face. And I was so mad, because he did seem to like her at first.

So then while Nathan was climbing over the white-painted three-plank fence and running away yelling something over his shoulder, and my mama and Aunt Millie were tumbling out and down the back porch steps to see what was happening out there, I was trying to wipe the watery grass clippings off my Loretta Young paper doll's warping sad face. She would never look the same again. I started to cry, and then I yelled, "Nathan, I'm gonna get you!" and my mama said from out in the yard, "Well, we can always buy another one." That was after she'd yelled at Nathan that next time he could play over here right or not at all. She was always telling him that, but even though I could see that he did try, it never lasted for very long. Aunt Millie came running all the way out to me in the yard and took that Loretta Young in her hand, smoothing and blotting and examining it, saying she'd bet it could be fixed up just fine. I of course said that I didn't want another one, but that I wanted that one. And no matter how nice and sweet Aunt Millie was, I knew I didn't want this one to have some new painted-on face, either.

Aunt Dorothy watched us coming back from the window, and then inside, the ladies went on back to the bridge table, where from the kitchen I could hear Aunt Celeste saying, "Are we playing bridge, or what?" On the kitchen floor I could see the Loretta Young had no chance now of ever being any dream-girl Miss America. Her whole face looked blotched and distorted now, the eyes puffed and faded, the mouth crooked, her paper-doll body blighted with stains—she looked as though she'd been forsaken in some back yard for years—neglected, unloved. I stretched out on the linoleum floor beside her. Then Aunt Millie, who was dummy in the game again, I guess, came in and looked and looked at both me and that Loretta Young. And then she said that we should have a nice funeral for Loretta Young and bury her out in the yard like they had done their cat that summer when it died of worms. Except of course it would be different, she said.

So then, even though I knew I wouldn't really get my daddy to dig a hole for putting it in the ground, I let my Aunt Millie go on and find a shoebox, while I laid out all the Loretta Young clothes that wouldn't work anyway for the Myrna Loy or the Betty Hutton—the skirts and sweaters and scarves and gloves and shoes and hats—all on the bed in little arrangements as they would have been worn in the Loretta Young dream-girl Miss America life, as it would have been if all this had never happened. Aunt Millie wanted to repaint the face for the funeral, like with the smiling Crayola lips, but I said no. Then even though I knew I was going to hide that boxed Loretta Young in my room in the bottom of my closet all covered up with shoes, so I could keep going in there and looking at her for years to come, I folded the tissue paper with Aunt Millie and then laid it and all the clothes into the box one by one alongside of the Loretta Young after we had put her in her favorite outfit. Then I laid in the cotton pads for the pink mink coat and hat to match, and Aunt Millie and I looked in the box at what we had done, and Aunt Millie said, "We are gathered together to say goodbye to a dear friend." And she carefully placed two pieces of honeysuckle on either side of the Loretta Young. Then she looked at me. I said, "She was the most beautiful and the nicest of them all." And I arranged four pearl buttons from my grandmother's house in the four corners of the shoebox. Then Aunt Millie said, "But bad things

THE QUARTERLY

happened to this Loretta Young that weren't her own fault."
Then she tossed up some M&Ms from the bridge-club game
so that they fell and bounced in the box like little confettis.
Then I brought out my mama's bottle of Shocking and we put
sprinkles of it all over ourselves and each other and that
Loretta Young. Then I said, "Amen." Then we closed up the
box without speaking or looking at each other, and Aunt Millie
went back into the living room and back to the game, while I
carried that boxed Loretta Young back into my room. But
before I hid it deep in the back of my closet, where no one
would ever find it, I took a last look at the poor wrecked face
with the light falling across it just so, and I very carefully drew
new red-pencil smiling lips turning just a little bit up at the
ends. And then I dropped in, crushing them, some soft sweet
white petals, just the same way my mama had once told me she
drove a man crazy by eating her gardenia corsage—petal by
petal by petal by petal . . . Amen. **Q**

The Honor System

Where Catherine and I first bumped into each other—where she backed into me—was on a shadowless expanse of desert floor in Death Valley National Monument, probably sixty miles' clearance in any direction. Friends consider this a new standard of clumsiness. They ask if it was tourist season, try to form pictures of foot traffic. It wasn't tourist season. This was at Badwater (Lowest Point in the Western Hemisphere), a crusty green pool that shrinks optically by fantastic degrees the closer you approach from the hills. It disappointed waves of nineteenth-century prospectors making the tearful, weaving descent to what had promised to be a stupendous reservoir of blue.

Today a highway stretches by the site to the turnout where Catherine's station wagon from DON GARP STUDIO CITY sat cooling its engine noisily, a crystal pot under the hood. In front of the car, a wooden information post in the style of a birdhouse offered Department of the Interior historical pamphlets for 50 cents on the honor system. That proposition had Catherine literally swaying. She had only a five-dollar bill; she wanted a pamphlet very much. You wondered if similar ethical questions had given her trouble in Studio City. You wondered things like that in Death Valley, because there was time to imagine the stories behind people. The truth was, Catherine had left Studio City in a divorcee trance—grabbing on to the first inspiration that came, which was that manners were going to exempt her from the ambiguities of life and distance would keep her out of "situations" somehow. She'd ironed all her dresses in a single evening and for two days had been touring Death Valley in a variety of them, smoothing creases. Finally, she made it to Badwater and got herself hypnotized by this 50¢ DONATION sign, which is where I found her when I arrived second in line. It sounds ridiculous, but that is how we were: Catherine behind dark glasses, breathing these high, swaying breaths, and me waiting my turn, dismally. Until at some point she wasn't swaying so much as backpedaling; I had to say "Whoa," as a warning, and our feet got tangled up.

Saying "Whoa" instead of "I'm sorry" is something my Westwood therapist would call growth. I'm more skeptical about it. I felt sorry the way men habitually feel sorry, part of a consciousness of being clumsy around facts of suffering; learning a new noise to make before falling down doesn't seem like big growth to me. How funny the fall must have looked— two people basically sitting down with a backward running start, Catherine throwing her handbag up in the air like a pizza—occurred to me belatedly. Nowadays I can laugh picturing it. I can divide it into its phases. It seems to me every fall has one truly great moment, a kind of awakening: you hit dirt and lie there a second, and the planetary silliness of everything comes up with the ground. That was when Catherine pushed her sunglasses back and blinked up at me like a screen star, for laughs, playing a scene about someone falling into someone's arms; I flashed back to a childhood game, the one where you fall down on purpose, and I wanted to fall again. But I didn't say so, and in the next interval I couldn't have known *how* to; we remembered we were strangers. You could see this realization come over Catherine, too. She stopped fluttering her eyes, because the screen-star bit hadn't gotten a laugh. She then hid her face in her hands and pretended to gag. She was on her elbows, next to me. This all happened in a second or two.

"No," I said. "It was very funny."

"What?" She looked at me. "Oh."

I wasn't sure we'd even understood each other. I looked away, feeling foolish.

"Oh, God," she said suddenly. Her eye picked out a loose thread on her dress and she broke it off, started smoothing some creases, and gave up. Then she slid herself back to a position against the base of the information post, with her head propped back, mock-seductively. She was acting again, playing someone whose bell had really been rung. She took an elaborate, heartsick breath and smiled. "Well—goodbye."

What was I supposed to say? It was one routine after another. My father views that sort of person as a "type"—the "type who's afraid you'll leave before they think of what they wanted to say" is how he puts it. At which I roll my eyes, if only by habit; I want that sort of insight to come from someone I have more in common with, like my sister, the screenwriter. But conversations with my sister only turn out wishful: we fantasize people into the mysteries we want them to be, fearless and unknowable, parentless. It frightens me to admit that my father's is the more loving view of human nature; I have no idea how he came to it. I took a pamphlet and walked past Catherine, to the edge of the pond, pretending to study the insect life under the surface. ("The wigglers are the larvae of the Soldier Fly.") Sunset was crossing the valley a hue at a time, and I stood there until I heard Catherine drive away.

My father is also my boss. He is the only surviving swimming-pool contractor on Ventura Boulevard in Sherman Oaks, which used to be the capital of the business, wall-to-wall showrooms. Now he stands at the window and points at the boulevard with his mug of chicken soup. "That's where National Pool was," he will say, "before it folded in '66." They *all* folded in '66; it was the year my father scored his knockout punch. He'd been a landscape architect for Artists' Pool and Patio (today Artists' Patio) and noticed something everyone else missed, which was that all the pools in the San Fernando Valley were virtually touching each other. (He was on an airplane at the time.) The only markets left to expand into were hillsides and custom improvements, which coincidentally were my father's twin loves at the drawing board: stainless-steel pools, pools shaped like highball glasses, pools on stilts, canyon feats. Within ten months, the entire industry fell to him like spilled poker chips. He hired all the out-of-work architects, and there's been little for him to do since. I am being groomed to inherit the business. I stand at the window next to him for as long as I can take it and then tell him I think I'll take a few days off and go to Death Valley, probably my third time in a month. He doesn't seem to care. He reminds me to "look up Ed Gurstone" for him. It's the same conversation every time; my father has never even *met* Ed Gurstone, but according to a computer printout of his, they are both Lainie Kazan Fan Club chapter presidents, with Ed holding down Death Valley. Not even an address given, just the chapter name: the 4,000-Foot Club. I tell my father I think it's pointless, but he won't listen; he is convinced Ed Gurstone is out there. By now, he has me conditioned. I will be driving up an absolutely barren incline, pass a sign that says ELEVATION 3,900 FEET, and a voice in my head will say, "Slow down."

I've domesticated Death Valley with my routines—a place to sleep, a place to drink my coffee, a place to read, traveling from one simpleminded station to the next, a toy train set on a billiard table. Of course, nothing is sacred about this program except to me. It's possible to share the same valley and carry an entirely different map. One afternoon I was packing my car and saw from the road a German man with zinc oxide on his nose positioning his wife for a snapshot on the sand dunes—the Place Where I Sleep. But how were they to know that? Every night I throw down my bedding there, wake up at seven exactly, see the faces of the dunes stitched with the tracks of sidewinders. Every morning for one dollar I shower by the Amigos Campground swimming pool, tiptoe over fishy puddles chowdered with toilet paper, comb my hair in the scored mirror over the sink. The place where I pray faces a jet-black hill covered with milky tumbleweeds—white-on-black, stunned, like an X-ray photograph. My second sighting of Catherine was at this spot. I found it one day after Badwater. It had seemed at once a mountain and its own afterimage; I saw it with my mind's eye and I could hit it with a stone. The effect was supernatural. I looked back at my footprints and the tire marks beyond them, and saw for the first time that the desert held a record of me, and always would, that there was no escaping my tracks, that I was either graceful or I wasn't; and in that instant of neutrality, I guessed that I was. For an abstract idea it came to me pretty literally. I spent the next half hour clomping around in circles, admiring my own steps. I stretched my fingers out at the sky. I lined up objects in my view, pretending I could blast them with a look; my eyes ran a line a mile long, over the highway and the salt flats and a dry riverbed, and then straight into the last thing I expected to see, specifically Catherine's sunglasses.

The instant of recognition startled the hell out of us both. In fact, I thought I could see her shudder, if you can see a shudder from the better part of a mile—it may have been a shadow, passing fast from a plane. Or it may have been nothing, just imagination, and my next thought was that Catherine couldn't see me at all, that her eyes were fixed miles past me on a mirage, or straight down at a snake—possibilities that went down with a single stroke when Catherine crossed her heels and, smoothly, curtsied. At me. She held the curtsy a long time, while I waved my Dodgers cap in salute, and when it ended, I went off, tossing the cap up and down all the way to my car.

That seemed to begin a flirtation. A strange one, considering the distances involved. Sometimes we would signal with a flash of headlights. Sometimes I would watch Catherine's station wagon reflecting the sun, sliding down a mountain road like a flame on a slow fuse. We did everything but come close enough to talk. We played gunfighters at five hundred yards, hands on holsters. We played photographers, Catherine advancing in a crouch, holding her sunglasses across her eyes like an Instamatic (a routine that was murder on her creases). A couple of days of this and I began to sleep badly. I would wonder what was going to come next in the game—staging scenes, resenting myself for devoting so much apparently romantic thought where there was so little basis. I would curse and try to sleep on my other side.

Then I would find myself replaying our first meeting. That Catherine and I met the way we did appealed to me for superstitious reasons. One, it was what the movie industry calls a "cute meet," which meant to me that we were destined to be together. We owed it to the movies. Two, lovers who met that way were nicely unprepared—having no chance to arrange themselves in the mirror of their fears. Here the realization that I had just thought my father's thought turned me over on my other side again. Whether real love was involved at all in my thoughts about Catherine I couldn't say. Once, when I was driving back from Scotty's Castle, in the northern hills, I heard a radio therapist say there was no such thing as "growing to love." Only I didn't get to hear the concept he came up with to replace it. He was using a myth-versus-fact style of presentation, and he was shouting, "There—is—no—such—thing—as—'growing—to—love' (interminable pause). . . . I'll say it again." The program was called *The Mental Health Hour.* Talk Radio is big for some reason in Death Valley, despite some primitive production values and despite the fact that there is virtually no audience here to phone in. Which leaves the therapist pretty much to his own rhythms, save for a sound engineer who likes to fill the silences with a tape recording of pounding surf. Little thought has been given to how idiotic pounding surf sounds in Death Valley; we get wave after wave. My problem this day was the mountain terrain: every time I rounded a curve, I lost the signal in the rocks. ". . . Lesson is this: Whomsoever you love," the man said—it was a favorite word of his, "whomsoever"—and then I would round a canyon wall and hit dead air. "Whomsoever, whomsoever, whomsoever!" And then, snowbanks of silence. Whomsoever I love, what? I was counting on reaching some open stretch of land at the critical moment of his thesis. As it happened, my car flew at the critical moment into a deep neck of road that may once have been a Borax mine. No daylight in sight. I made a desperate

three-point turn and tried to get back to where I'd been, sliced
the radio needle back and forth across the band, but never
recovered the voice. At a turnout at the top of the hill, ten
thousand feet up, where it is cold, I parked my car and stood
in a stiff wind to stare across the valley; instantly this hit me
as a trite pose, my hands in the pockets of my parka, and my
heartsick sigh, like Catherine's heartsick sigh at Badwater, the
difference being that hers was intended for a laugh. Over all
of these things I lost sleep. Our every posture seemed inordi-
nately important. The valley enlarged small lives.

Finally, I saw Catherine up close again. By accident.
With just enough time gone by for me to have worked up a
personal sense of ultimatum, of what-gives? Catherine was
towel-drying her hair at the washbasin by the pool at Amigos
Campground, around noon on a Sunday, and when she saw
me, she got cute right away. She shook her wet hair down over
her eyes. "Small world," she said. "Question mark."

I nodded. Some teenagers who work at the ranch were
drinking beers in the shallow end of the pool. German men
bobbed in the deep end (German tourists love the American
West), their gawky, topless wives reading novels in chaises by
the Coke machine. Catherine was not topless. She wore a
green bikini under a man's dress shirt and, without even stop-
ping to think, I asked her, "Whose shirt?"

She blushed.

"Never mind," I said. "I'm sorry."

"This shirt?" she said. "This shirt belongs to a wealthy
man who says I remind him of the girl who baby-sat him when
he was a boy in Morocco." She snapped shut a compact mirror
and looked me in the eye. "It's my husband's shirt. Ex-
husband's. And I'd forgotten the association. You could have
asked me anything else and the subject would never have come
up." She looked down and, when she raised her eyes again, she
shook a finger at me. "So, nice going."

And then we were quiet, while I watched her at the mirror.

She buttoned up the shirt, slipped out of her bathing-suit top from inside, and stashed it in a beach bag, both of us trying to act very modern and indifferent, and failing; finally, she let out all her air at once and had to lean on the basin with her forearms.

"Why are you so bold with me when you're far away?" I said.

"Why are *you*?"

"Well, I'm willing to get to know you right here."

She coughed. "Oh. Until *I* am, you mean. I mean, how convenient a thing for you to say when I'm already walking away. You know?"

"Huh?" I said.

"Let's understand each other. You're beginning to have a crush on me."

I shifted my weight onto the other foot and a few seconds went by and I shifted my weight back onto the original foot. "No, I'm not," I said.

She made a hopeless expression. "You *act* like you are," she explained. "You smile constantly. Without even blinking. You wave that . . . *cap.*"

"You started it!" I said. "It's a Dodgers hat."

"And boy, oh boy, you ran with it."

"So?"

"So!" She buried her face in her hands. She looked up suddenly, pained. "It really smells in here." And she whirled off to the pool, past it; I swept back one side of my hair in the mirror and took off behind her. She kept twenty yards between us. I walked faster. She walked faster. She entered the camp cafeteria, passed rows of green Jell-O in a trot; I trotted past green Jell-O. She zigzagged through the aisles and the tables, and had me good and beat when she reached the far door, put a hand on it, and looked up at the sign above, EMERGENCY EXIT ONLY. And froze. I caught up, and she hung her head.

So we went for a walk, beyond the camper stalls, toward the road. A hot wind had come up, bullying the sides of tents.

Here Catherine told me about her Studio City life and told me her name and told me that her approach with a man had always been to play coy and lead him along, later to call his bluff by pointing out that he was mainly addicted to the chase, the same as she was. The routine afforded each of Catherine's men a graceful and dramatic exit. By the time she met Ramsey, she thought it was foolproof, and was getting extravagant with her goodbyes. "I'm saying goodbye to someone I could spend my life with," Ramsey had said to her. And she replied, "If only you'd told me." They shook hands, and then he hung on to her hand for a moment and said, "Well, *I'm telling you.*" They stood there and then embraced, miserably, each realizing the gravity of the mistake. She had no idea how she was going to hold his interest now. In a wedding picture taken just after the pronouncement and the kiss, both their mouths hung wide. From there, they went on what seemed like an ironic vacation: a honeymoon to try and patch things up. On the first night, Catherine danced ten dances with a college freshman and Ramsey slept with an actress. Finally, they had a dramatic goodbye that stuck. (Ramsey said, "I love you too much to put you through this.")

That was six months ago, Catherine said. She assured me that if I had a crush on her, it was only a crush on her "act," because what else did I have to go on? Her own question incited her. What the hell else do you have to go on? she said, and then clutched her stomach. She was nauseous. It had started at the washbasin and gradually got worse; when she finished sentences now, she was adding the comment "—dizzy." At which we both had to pause, there in the driveway, wind rattling the campground gate. "I'll be all right when we get to the highway," she said. "These faces dancing around. It's like in a telephoto lens."

At the highway, she was not all right. At the highway, it was chaos—the illness and the wind outdoing each other, a hysterical duet. Catherine walked backward, with her arms folded under her ribs; I trudged toward her through sheets of sand that raced by, strobe-lighting the highway; a thick beige dust from the valley floor was swelling at the horizon like bread. We were having a civilized argument: I kept yelling, asking why Catherine wouldn't stand still for two seconds so I could catch up, and Catherine kept yelling, asking what I thought love was. Specifically, Catherine's argument was that you could not love a person when you hadn't seen the "real" person, and my argument was, didn't she think it worked the other way around: that love came first, and then if you were open to the idea, love automatically saw through to the "real" person, the person it intended to love. She stared at me, fighting to keep her shirt flat. "Whomsoever," I said. I was gesturing at clouds.

"You're really full of it," she said finally.

Some sand lashed my cheeks. "Wait up!" I called.

She pointed across the road. "We can talk in my car!"

"What about your stomach?"

She searched around with her fingers for pain, looked at me. She shrugged.

Ed Gurstone is a stout, pink-faced man with smooth white hair firmed back in rows, like a half dozen ladyfingers. Not that I had any idea in advance what the man was supposed to look like. It was his Winnebago that identified him for me. Catherine and I had ducked into her station wagon to talk, and then more or less noticed we didn't need to; our willingness to resolve things was as good as having done it. We just held hands in the front seat with our eyes closed, reliving what had happened already. Listening to sand sprinkle the windshield. Suddenly I had an intuition and opened my eyes. In the rear-view I saw it: a wide-load motor home straining around a bend, in that harried, anthropomorphic way that motor homes strain around bends; then it barreled down the straightaway, close enough for me to make out the bullhorns on the roof and the hot-red lettering across the front: L-A-I-N-I-E. I practically threw myself under the wheels flagging him down.

A lot of shouted apologies and running about, and finally

Gurstone helped us inside. He didn't share my sense of emergency about the errand, but he was polite. He made coffee and wrote down a P.O. box number to give to my father. From then on, the three of us just sipped coffee, staring out of opposite windows, trying to think of something to talk about. "I imagine it simplifies things, being the only member of the 4,000-Foot Club," I said, all of us nodding; Gurstone thought for several seconds and finally turned out his palms. "Well, the buck stops here!" he said. He exploded with laughter. A second later, we were all sipping our coffees and gazing in opposite directions again. "I used to live in town," Gurstone said. "But living here keeps things basic. I'm a remedial sort of person."

So am I, and Death Valley is always teaching me one lesson or another—though recently picturing the desert has had to take the place of going there. That is a good sign. It shows, for one thing, that my job has become tolerable to me; I've even started to put some imagination into it. Promotions and things. The county-museum tribute to pool culture this year—that was my own idea. Also, I've been handing my father a series of preposterous landscaping challenges, which have put him back at the drawing board, with his Walkman on, late into the night. I see Catherine most nights. We're "dating," but taking slow steps, for her sake. She is more cautious about involvements than I am. Here is where my memories of Death Valley serve me well. I picture us at Badwater, where things are so irreducible: Catherine and me and the land, and my superstitions of destiny—Gurstone is the wild card in this arrangement, his Winnebago careening sometimes into view, across the background, at the instant of our fall. It is as if my involvement with Catherine began at the ending, the essence—a notion that lifts me again and again to feelings of good faith. We almost never fight. Catherine might make us late for a movie, say, by taking too long to iron a dress—and instead of getting irritated about it, I'll simply think, Badwater. Then things blow over. It is a practical aid to life. **Q**

Those Twisting Things

It was the worst divorce in the history of the world. Besides the BMW, house, children, and dog—besides the furniture, tennis racquets, refrigerator, and VCR—Vern also had to ride around town once a week, strapped to the hood of the station wagon like a deer, stripped to his boxer shorts, with Sue driving, honking and waving. It was part of the settlement; it was what she wanted, and she'd gotten it.

She'd take her time about it, driving slowly down the wide center of Capitol Street at lunchtime, as if leading a parade: and everyone who worked in the office with Vern, and, in fact, everyone in the city of Jackson—people over in the Standard Life building even, with binoculars—could look down and see him—silent, suffering, thinking about something. Like most people's, Vern's brow furrowed when he was thinking, and he looked captured and aboriginal, down there like that, almost naked, and frowning—and Vern and Sue's children, as part of the judgment, got to ride along in the station wagon and eat ice cream, with the air conditioner blowing. They would be laughing, because it *was* funny—even Vern had to admit it was funny; and because it made the children laugh, Vern let Sue keep doing it, once a week.

There was this one dresser he wanted, after the divorce—one he'd had since high school—a horrible, chocolate-colored, splintery old thing, worth nothing, worth absolutely nothing, but he thought it would fit in this one small corner he had, in his apartment, and so he asked Sue for that, at least.

But she narrowed her already small and deep-set eyes and said, "No." I was there, and I heard it, saw it, saw how she closed her eyes when she said "No," and it was exactly the way some women do when they close their eyes and whisper "Yes," at the right moment.

When Vern first signed up for the divorce, he had thought that he would be able to move to a beach, start living in a grass hut, sleep late, do some cooking, some beachcombing: go for a dip around noon every day—but instead, the judge ended up ordering him to ride around on top of the station wagon, and also to go out and start making even more money than he already had been, and to give all of it to his wife—she would see that the children got it—and so, because he did not have the BMW, Vern would ride his bike to work—twelve miles each way—and he'd bathe under his arms up in the men's room with a dampened brown paper towel, after his arrival each morning. He kept his grungy old tennis shoes, his dirty old jock, in his lower desk drawer. Wore a tie, presented a smile to businessmen coming in and out of his office.

"An animal," he'd tell me, staring into his beer after work: down in that dark owl of a dungeon bar, happy hour—and outside, the time of his divorce, gorgeous fall, hard October light, people walking past, leaves tumbling, places to go, people with a life still to be lived. "Just an animal," he'd mourn.

I'd be very uncomfortable, listening to it, and would be anxious to get outside, back into the light. I wanted to go hit some tennis balls, or go for a run on the levee; or I wanted to go for a walk by myself, or wash the car, or paint the mailbox. I'd been thinking about taking flying lessons, too, and some weekends I'd drive out to Hawkins Field and watch the little planes practicing, coming down in wavers and slides, floating, bouncing when they hit, aiming for the runway with no confidence but much determination; trying to get it right. Or I'd think of how I could go fishing out on the lake with my girl-friend, whom I'd been dating for twelve years, and whom I almost certainly never was going to marry.

To tell you the truth, I'd already been out to Hawkins Field a few times—I mean to the little metal trailer house where they taught ground school and gave flying lessons; and I'd even gone so far, one wild day, as to give the instructor twenty bucks to take me up for half an hour.

It seemed that it went by so fast. We were barely up in the air and away from the city—I was craning my head to look back at the sloppy river that runs through our town flooding and often causing bad smells and always looking sullen and unexciting—the Pearl, what a name—and I was trying to pick out the building in which I worked every day, trying to see if, from the air, it was taller and more magnificent than all the other surrounding buildings—and then the pilot—a really young kid, maybe still even a teenager, with dirty yellow hair to his shoulders and aviator sunglasses, a baseball cap—like a madman, he grabbed my arm and pretended to be having a heart attack.

It scared me very badly. I'm afraid that I behaved poorly.

I unbuckled my harness and leaned across and grabbed him by his neck.

"You son of a *bitch*!" I shrieked. His eyes were wide, behind the green sunglasses, and he looked really, really frightened; this at six thousand feet. I'm sure my own face was all twisted up and red, pretty frightening itself. I felt weightless, as if nothing I did would matter. "You know I don't know how to fly this thing, you moon-faced son of a bitch!" I started shaking him back and forth in his seat—our plane was banking, flying all wrong—and he shrugged free, pulled away quickly, and took the controls again.

I settled back into my seat, and we made a turn and descended. He said something into the microphone, into the radio. He looked around for other traffic, meekly. He was being perfect.

Closer in to Jackson, and a little closer to the ground, I felt better, even wild again, bold.

I reached in my wallet and gave him another twenty dollars.

"Do some rolls," I said. "And some of those twisting things."

Like a crazy man, I held my hand out and pretended that it was the plane, and showed him the loopy things I wanted it to do; I made the sound I thought the plane would make, like a child, as my hand fluttered all around, diving and climbing: "Nee-yeee-owwww . . ."

I was acting like a crazy man.

Vern was somewhere down there! Remember Vern! I certainly did.

"We've got to get down," said the pilot. "We don't have much gas."

But I wouldn't hear of it.

"Do some fancy stuff," I said, almost pleading. We were getting really close to the runway, sinking on a bed of hot mushy air, and I was almost frantic.

"Please," I said. "Anything." **Q**

Spending the Day with Donald Trump

All the way to her address I see dead dogs by the roadside. The papers say somebody from somewhere has been addicted, has deposited the poisoned things up and down the tree-lined road, at the entranceway to an acre and a half of house, in front of a bank or church, behind the rear wheel of a Rolls. Whether it means anything or not is the ten-thousand-dollar question. That's the reward. In this neighborhood a pedigreed dog gets a burial and a tombstone. At her address they put flowers on the graves of dogs.

The local cops are shaking the ivy, after the culprit. I pull past the mansion, which nestles in a circle of trees a long way from the street, and park in the circular drive. Without knocking, I enter, a briefcase of tools with me. "Man in the hallway! Man in the hallway!" I shout, climbing the stairs. The bathroom door at the end of the hallway is closed. I imagine lace panties. "Typewriter man!" I scream again, taking no chances. At her door, I rap like Woody Woodpecker.

She opens it, rubbing her Irish eyes until they're full of freckles. She thinks she can hear me, see me full way round, only I'm looking at myself through her eyes, the way I'm bunched up inside my pants, the way my eyes go glassy and distant when I'm aroused, the way I reach for myself. At dinner, she'll tell them, all those people who come here every few weeks and talk as food is placed before them, that I'm only twenty years out of date. She'll call me eccentric, guess about my toupee. But she won't tell them what my head looks like without the hair. She won't tell them what I keep in my pockets.

"I've developed a relationship with this typewriter," she says, motioning me to her cubbyhole. "If you can fix it, whack

it and get it going again, I'd certainly show my appreciation."
It's an unhealthy relationship, I think about saying, but I smile
brightly. "Trouble is," she continues, "it won't go. In Ireland,
we don't have electric typewriters." She pauses and hears what
she's saying. I'm getting ideas about an overseas franchise. "At
least I don't. So when this one doesn't go, you see, I think it's
me. But it's not. It's plugged in, you see, it's turned on. It
hums, but often it won't go. It's defective."

"Let me have a look, lassie," I say in my best brogue.
"Sometimes a good whack in the potato is all a thing needs,
you're right about that, but the world is more technical than
you imagine. You never know what might come crawling
through your window." She'll imitate that brogue over coffee
in the breakfast room, only she won't describe the way flea
powder replaces talc, how it tickles the nose. I tinker here,
tinker there, caressing the machine, keeping up the chatter.
Now is the time for all good men to come to the aid of their party, I type.
The *y* leaps off the page.

"It's not stuck, you see," she says. "When it works, it
doesn't quite."

"Yes. Believe me, lassie, I know typewriters. This needs
the shop. We'll get you another." They come from anywhere,
by invitation, to the mansion, deeded for the good of literature
in a dead man's will. I knew that dead man before he was dead.
I expected he would leave a little something to me because I
did him favors, brought him all sorts of treats he couldn't get
anywhere else. He lived alone except for the help, but often
enough, his city friends stayed somewhere on the premises.
When he took sick and died, what he left me was trade.

When I first brought the Irish one her typewriter, a Swik-
swatch, sleek and Oriental, I gave her a wink. "What do you
people really do here?" I said. She would retell that one, too,
but after my question her eyes fluttered. She was stuck for a
smart reply. There was no lock on her door, I noticed, no
chain. Outside her vine-covered window, the roof sloped like

a woolly mammoth almost to the garden, where there were benches and chairs. I knew after dark there were no garden lights. "You from Ireland?" I asked, letting her off the hook.

"Yes, Kilkenny," she said, absolutely polite, suddenly a bit frightened. I was the real thing, you see. I was what everyone talked about over there, a real American man, real enough to knock her flat.

"Yeah? You must be really glad to get away from all those bombs."

All the way back to my shop I could imagine her getting her money's worth out of that one. "Ireland to his mind is this little lay-by where everyone's ducking bombs." People should take advantage of what they have. Sure enough, I thought, locking the shop and preparing my solution—bane of dog, hair of woman, gland of frog. And then the assorted drugs. I know enough about drugs to be a pharmacist.

But some people have too much. I drive down these streets, see houses big enough for half of Oakland to live in. They're hidden behind clipped hedges, behind a Sherwood Forest of trees, all protected by elaborate security and Dobermans, all manicured by truckloads of maintenance men, little Mexicans who get peanuts, all patted down by interior designers, cooks, servants, dog shrinks. I know these people think they can do whatever they want. All those rooms, all those closed doors.

You live in a duplex without a yard, everybody knows your business—when your old man comes home drunk, when he takes out the strap. You live in a castle, people imagine *Dallas* or *Dynasty,* even in a geriatric ward like this one, where people get to be thirty and look as if their lives are over. I got screwed up before I could come into my own, I'm not so crazy I don't know that. What I had got lost. The Irish lass, she has a sense of humor so that what she takes advantage of gives pleasure. We're much alike, she and I. We deserve a night together.

But take Donald Trump. He has friends down the street. I read about him in the papers, all that property, all that money. Stretch limos, cellular phones, computers instead of armrests. I studied the man when he owned that New Jersey football team.

"What you writing, lassie, a play?" I ask, hefting the replacement, an old faithful Selectric, into the cubbyhole beside the shelf: tin can of ink pens, stack of bond paper, note cards with illegible scribble, Tylenol, vitamin pills, alarm clock, books.

"You must be a prognosticator," she says. "You're exactly right."

She's flirting, and I tease from her when she goes to sleep, what kind of schedule the house keeps.

"Let me guess," I say in my brogue. "It's a play about women and firecrackers and the Fourth of July, three things that go together like Mom, the flag, and apple pie."

She smiles brightly. I've overdone it; she walks clear round me, sees me from several sides. I almost give it away. "Well, it's a voice play," she finally says. "It's not exactly about anything. Oh, that's not right. Maybe it's about the things we lose. It's sort of performance art. You know, Philip Glass, David Byrne, Robert Wilson? *Koyaanisqatsi, The Knee Plays, The Catherine Wheel?* You try to hear a voice to get it down, then the interplay of voices, then a kind of sound track."

I shrug. "People should take advantage of what they have. Performance art, that's like all the dead dogs around the village, right? I mean, photograph them, write about them, maybe get a statement from the culprit for the museum wall, do a mug shot. Maybe look at the culprit's diary or his altar."

"That's a little extreme, wouldn't you say so?" she asks uneasily.

At least she's heard about the dogs. "Like the Irish bombs, then?"

"Okay, then, like the bombs, if you insist."

"You want to hear voices," I say, "you ought to do like that woman. She speaks for some guy, Ramses or something, who's 35,000 years old. He lives on a mountain in Tibet. She gets into a trance and comes on in a deep voice, very seductive. She makes a mint. Hauls them in with a hook, all the yoyos."

"Yes, well, each to her own," she says primly. "You seem to know a lot about it."

"I keep my eyes open. I pay attention." I can see I'm wearing out my welcome. "But you're right. It all comes out in the wash. Try the thing out," I say, pointing.

She pecks at it. There's a porcelain knob beneath a mirror nailed above her small bureau. On the knob she's hung some jewelry: a pearl necklace, a turquoise bracelet.

I'm edging from the room now, my hand deep in one pocket. She's hearing me with only one ear; she's already developing a relationship with the Selectric. "I'd give Donald Trump my dough, but on one condition only. I don't have to *see* the man, I don't have to *talk* to the man, I don't have to *think about* the man. Let the man do his thing, but keep him off the grass."

The next morning there's a dead dog on the front stoop.

I can see how it plays. She stares at the typewriter. During the night somebody touched her, there was something in her mouth. She may have been dreaming, she may have been drugged. She can't quite remember, her blood is heavy. Some jewelry seems to be misplaced, but maybe she left it back home. There's a kind of suction-feel to her pucker, no taste when she eats toast. She's not sure whom to tell what to. She sits in the kitchen for hours with cold coffee, willing to listen to anything, anyone, marking time until the dinner bell. She blames it on her new typewriter. **Q**

Minnows

The mother lived on a lake. It was a clean lake. Many people came to the lake to swim and fish. It was past summer now. There were a few people who lived on the lake, but now most of them were gone for the winter. It was fall. The grass was dry around the mother's house. The road that went around the lake was unpaved. The dirt was dry. When a car drove by, the dirt went up into the air. There were birches around the lake. They were slender and white, and their leaves turned yellow in the fall. It was a sunny day this day. The mother was expecting her daughter. The mother took sandwiches out of the refrigerator and put them on the kitchen table. The mother had cleaned the house. She had worked hard cleaning the house, because the house was already clean. The mother wanted the house to be clean in her mind.

But the daughter was with two boys when she arrived. They were just a little older than the daughter. They had hair on their chins, but it was not much hair. They had pulled up in a blue Cadillac. The car was rusted. It made a great deal of noise. The dust from the road hung in the air. The girl had been driving. She let the boys get out first. The boys came up the flagstone walk and introduced themselves. The mother smiled. She just wanted to see her daughter, but she smiled to please the two boys. They seemed like good boys. But actually one of them had long hair. It fell across his eyes. The other had neater hair. But there seemed to be something mischievous about these boys. The daughter said the boys were staying for only a short time.

It was a nice day out. It was dry. The water in the lake was warm even though it was September. The daughter went in ahead of the mother so that the mother would see her long braid.

The boys did not eat the sandwiches. The mother offered them some, but the boys said they had eaten already. She offered to make them more sandwiches, to make different kinds, but the boys said they didn't want any. One of the boys stood up while the mother was still insisting. He went to the window that overlooked the lake. He looked down the dried lawn to the boat he saw turned upside down. He asked if he could take it out. She said okay. But it made her nervous to think of someone going out in the boat. It was just that she had been looking at the overturned boat for so long. Nobody had used it. It seemed right that nobody had used it. If somebody did, then things wouldn't remain as they were. It was a nice day, a much nicer day than usual. Why ruin it by having an accident? Why not leave the boat alone?

The mother told the boys to be careful. She looked out the window down the lawn to the lake. One boy took off his shirt. The other lit a cigarette and threw the match behind him. They looked dark and dirty. Their hair bounced as they went down the lawn. The mother turned back to her daughter. She wasn't going to watch them turn the boat over. She sat down at the table.

"I was wondering why you brought the boys," the mother said. "I mean, who are they? You haven't even told me who they are."

"I live with them," the daughter said.

"How is that, dear?" the mother said.

"I do it with them," the daughter said.

The mother stood up and went upstairs. The windows upstairs were open. The ceiling of her bedroom slanted down here because of the roof. The mother went to one of the windows and looked out. There were the boys in the boat. They were sitting in it making waves. She turned away and thought about what she usually did at this time of day. She took a cool bath. That would be the correct thing to do now, pretend it was as it had been. She brought a clean towel into the bathroom, locked both the doors, and got undressed. She had the water in the tub running. She put her fingers in it. Cooler or warmer? She tried to think which would be better for her heart. Cooler. She turned the faucet cooler. Then, when she put her foot in and found the water quite cool, she said to herself: "I'd better make it warmer."

She turned the hot water on. She kept it on for a moment without the cold. She moved her foot up the tub away from the faucet. The hot water steamed. She added some cool water and made it lukewarm. She added the lukewarm water until the water in the tub was the same temperature as the room. Then she put both legs in and adjusted the faucet. Cooler or warmer? she thought. She tried cooler and then sat down. That was right. That was fine. She made it a little more cool. Then she turned the faucet off. She could hear it dripping. She could hear the water in the tub as she moved her legs.

There were two doors to the bathroom. One was at the top of the stairs. The girl stood outside of this one.

"Who is it?" the mother asked.

"Me," the daughter said.

The mother knew it was her. Who else? The two boys were in the boat.

"What, dear?" the mother said. "I'm in the tub."

"You just left without saying where you were going," the daughter said.

"This is my bath time," the mother said.

The mother soaped herself under her arms. She had hair under her arms. She had let it grow ever since her husband had left her. She never saw anybody who would notice. Besides, she kept her legs shaved. Who would think she shaved her legs but not under her arms? She soaped the black hair under her arms.

"Mother, open up!" the daughter said.

"Your mother is taking a nice quiet bath," the mother said.

The mother looked at the ceiling, the porcelain sink, and the mirror. She turned the water on again. Had she ever had it this cold? Could her heart stand it? The water was up to her breasts. The daughter was outside the door, the two boys on the lake.

The mother stood up and took the towel from the rack. Her body was pink. She dried herself off. She stood for a moment holding the pink towel to her chest. Then she opened the cabinet behind the mirror and took out the talcum powder. She put the powder under her arms.

The mother went back down to her chair in the kitchen. Dried flowers were in a vase on the table. She looked out the window at the boat. It was the same as before they came. She couldn't tell the difference. It was quiet in the room. For a moment, she thought she would take her bath. Then she thought, How silly, I just took one.

There were no clouds in the sky. She got up from the table and went out the door down to the water. She was very dressed up. She stood by the water and looked down. She could see the sand under the water where the boys had walked up. In the sun, in the water, she could see the minnows swimming in different directions. **Q**

History

511, CLOVIS DIES.

Kathleen reads this silently; she has to twist in her seat to see the words. The timeline is stenciled high on the wall. Fluorescent light makes the blue letters gleam.

485, MEROVINGIAN FRANKS UNDER CLOVIS . . .

"Yes!" Mr. Mahajan says, looking up from his desk, his eye caught by the movement of Kathleen's hair, which is wild and curly and red, the same deep burnt red as the filaments of saffron that Sushila uses to tint the rice gold. The hair looks crinkly, like the saffron; it looks—but this is foolishness—expensive. "Yes," he says, less certainly, forgetting what he intended to say.

401, VISIGOTHS INVADE ITALY.

He stares at the textbook on his desk, open to pages 58, 59, the accounts of one R. Roberts appearing on the left; R. Roberts owns a cleaning establishment. Perhaps—his eyes shift to page 59, to the accounts of N. Lamb, internist. Dr. Lamb's figures are more complex, the capital and income statements more of a challenge. But American girls dislike a challenge. They quit coming to class when the work becomes difficult. In four weeks, twenty-six students have vanished— dropped out, he fears, though they all may be ill. Each Tuesday evening there have been fewer, until tonight there are only these four girls. It may be bad luck to take attendance; he's not sure the office requires it. There's no one in the office at night except a girl to answer the phone.

Sighing, he decides on R. Roberts. No, he will do Dr. Lamb. It's impossible to make bookkeeping simple; the most he can do is try to make it clear. Of course, he should have decided beforehand which exercise to put on the board, but Anil was fussing all through supper; the child has caught Sushila's cold. Soon, no doubt, he will catch it himself; the land-lord keeps the apartment too cool, barely 60 degrees in Anil's room, according to the thermometer hung on the crib. The electric heater has helped at night, but Anil might burn himself during the day.

286, DIOCLETIAN . . .

She likes these weird names: Diocletian, Pepin. There's Pepin the Younger and Pepin the Short. And Clovis—she likes that name, too, hates her own name: Kath*leen,* Kath*leen.* "Kath-leen, Kathleen," Mrs. Feldman calls up the stairs, and Kath-leen wants to quit on the spot, wants to go home and go back to bed, but of course she can't do that. "Kathleen, now, today, Kathleen, you'll remember about the dining-room window-sill?" Every single Friday it's the same thing, and it's just useless to try to explain. "But, Mrs. Feldman . . ." she says sometimes. Mrs. Feldman says, "I'm late, Kathleen," or "Not now," or "Don't argue with me," as if you could argue with Mrs. Feldman. It's not fair—you can't dust the windowsill un-less you move the artillery fern, and if you move the artillery fern, you have to put it back where it belongs. Only, if you so much as look at the fern, it's dropping these things like little brown seeds, so there's no way, ever, to prove that you dusted unless you put the fern somewhere else. And she tried that—left the fern on the dining table, in the center, under the chandelier, but the following Friday Mrs. Feldman said, "Kath-leen, I can't have that fern on the dining table." Kathleen would not have that fern in the house, but it was a present from the Feldmans' daughter, Rachel, pictures of whom Kathleen must dust; eighteen of them hang in the upstairs hall, and downstairs there are twelve pictures of grandchildren. What you do about pictures to prove you dusted: you always leave some of them hanging crooked. Then Mrs. Feldman says, "Re-ally, Kathleen! Try not to leave the pictures every which way." Mrs. Feldman is on Kathleen's hate list, just below a basset named Albert. Mr. Feldman is nice, though; he has a nice face. He's what you call a cantor in the Jewish church. He's home

a lot, because he's retired, but he always keeps out from underfoot. Most of the time, he goes to the cellar, and she can hear
him practicing his singing down there.

Tracy—she likes the name Tracy. Tracy Gordon sits in
front of her. They can sit any place they want, but she and
Tracy usually sit together, go outside at the break for a smoke.
Tracy's knitting a muffler—fuzzy, soft yarn, a lovely dark
green. Bob might like a muffler like that, if only Kathleen knew
how to knit. She glances at the clock. Ten of seven. In twenty
minutes she could have learned.

She glares at Mr. Mahajan, willing him to start teaching
something, but his pale brown face hovers close to the book;
he wears thick, heavy glasses, like binoculars. When he moves
his head slowly from side to side, a camera is what he reminds
her of, the kind they have on *Nature* or something, where
they're panning around the floor of the ocean. They're showing you white worms nine feet long, underwater volcanos making steam.

"Yes!" Mr. Mahajan says, pushing his chair back. "Let us
look at Dr. Lamb." He stands at the blackboard. "Where is my
chalk?" He had it, he knows, when he wrote *Chapter 4*. Then
what did he do? Sat down at his desk. He goes to the desk and
looks under the textbook; the chalk is nowhere in sight. Sushila says he is absentminded. For days he has neglected to call
the landlord, not forgotten exactly—he often remembers, but
not when he is anywhere near a phone. And he is entirely
within his rights: when the landlord supplies the heat, the
temperature at night must be 64. It is the law, Mary Mirsky
says. Mary Mirsky found a mistake in his work, a stupid mistake, a copying error. She said, "What's wrong with you, Ramesh? You haven't seemed your usual self." What is his usual
self? He checks and rechecks his work. He is known for his
accuracy, not for his speed. He must not make mistakes.

180, ROMANS DEFEATED IN SCOTLAND.

It's all defeats and invasions. Last week she learned the
parts of a castle from the poster that's tacked up next to the

blackboard. So now she knows about crenellations, and she knows this new word, "keep," but she doesn't know a whole lot about bookkeeping, only what she's learned from the book. *Stop,* it says. *Before you go on, do Exercise 4.1.* She does, not looking at the solution, which is printed right below. *Now check your work,* the book instructs, and she's usually got it right. But the teacher just copies from the book. He should make up some exercises himself. Plus, they're doing only one chapter a week, and there are eighteen chapters in the book. Four more classes, she paid fifty bucks. She's paying the teacher to look for chalk.

He runs his fingers along the chalk tray, his fingernails filling with powder and dust. No chalk. They should leave him more than one piece. The first evening, they left him none; he had to send a girl to the class next door. Borrowing—he is always having to borrow; he had to borrow to buy his car. And the car is always breaking down; he still has not had the defroster fixed. Some morning soon, there will be frost. Next month, there could be snow. Sushila says, "You work for a pittance. When are you going to ask for a raise?" And "When are they going to promote you? You should be head accountant." But Mary Mirsky is head accountant at the firm of Mirsky & Green. She will stay home, Sushila thinks, once she is pregnant, and then the job will be his. But Sushila is the one who is pregnant—and Anil not yet a year and three months. Anil's room is too small for two cribs, but how can they afford to move?

"Where is my chalk?" he cries, in Hindi, his voice sounding high and wild. The unhelpful girls stare back, giving no sign that they have heard. He must calm down, calm down and think. At the beginning of the evening, he had the chalk.

Kathleen knows the chalk's in his pocket. That is where he usually puts it: his pants pocket, in with his handkerchief; in his handkerchief pocket are pens and pencils. But she's not going to tell him, because she hates him; he's wasting so much of her time.

He reaches in for his handkerchief, to wipe the dirt from his fingertips, feels the chalk, but it's too late; he has already pulled out the handkerchief. And the chalk has leaped onto the floor, where it breaks in three pieces, none longer than a centimeter. He picks them all up—let the foolish girls giggle—and writes *31 December* on the board. The chalk scrapes, and the girls cry out, but he writes on, ignoring them: *Accounts Payable, Accounts Receivable (A/R).* He is whispering the amounts as he writes: *Miscellaneous Expense, Rent Expense, Rent Expense, Supplies Expense.*

"As of December 31," he turns to face them, relieved to find his voice under control, "the accounts of R. Roberts are as follows . . ." He reads the entire list out loud.

"He hasn't got a full deck," Tracy says, as they stand outside at the break. The end of her cigarette glows in the dark; when she takes a drag, her face looks mean. She has short blond hair, practically punk, left longer on top but not spiked. "I thought he was going to break down and cry."

Once when Kathleen was still in high school, the chemistry teacher did break down. He was drawing a blast furnace on the blackboard; then he muttered, "Who gives a shit?" Next thing they knew, he walked out of the room, and they got this substitute. Didn't know squat. It could happen again, she supposes. Mr. Mahajan wrote *Rent Expense* twice.

But Tracy is off on another tack. "I'm trying to keep my husband's books, right? It's not like I'm taking this class just for fun."

So who is? Kathleen thinks, and she's mad at Tracy, more like miffed, because Tracy thinks she's special or something; she's always saying "my husband." You don't see Tracy out cleaning houses, vacuuming dog hair off the sofas and wiping up where the dog has just pissed on the floor you washed an hour before. She gets to stay home with her little kid; her husband paid for the class.

"Payroll's Chapter 10," Tracy says, "and we aren't even going to get that far." But all Kathleen says is "Yeah"; she's biting her tongue not to say, "I could care." Rosario and Melinda come out just then, and Tracy says, "We should report him."

"Who?" says Melinda.

"Mr. Mahajan."

"Report him for what?" Rosario asks.

"Well, Jesus—for total incompetence."

Kathleen blows her smoke straight up. "He might be an okay accountant."

"Don't be an asshole," Tracy says, but Kathleen doesn't like that, either, calling her an asshole; she's feeling real prickly. She doesn't like the way Tracy laughs. "If we had to have an incompetent teacher, why did they have to give the job to a foreigner?"

Does that make sense? Kathleen thinks. She throws her cigarette onto the lawn. "I'm going to hit the ladies' room." She saunters off toward the building.

The rest room's clear down at the other end of the hall, like about the length of a football field, just before the exit to the parking lot; she might as well get in her car and drive home. Except her textbook is still lying on her desk—nine dollars she paid for that book, an hour and a half of taking shit. She doesn't dare go to the ladies' room. She'd walk out the door and never come back, plus she'd never read the book on her own. She stops at the drinking fountain instead.

"Next week," Mr. Mahajan says, "I think we must have an examination."

If he could take back the words, he would. Four pairs of eyes have gone narrow and fierce. But surely it is usual to test the students. Ah, but what use will it be? When he said, "What goes into the income statement?" they could not even say, "Income from fees." They needed only to refer to the book, but even that was asking too much. "Income from fees," he had to prompt, "yes?" Bored vacant eyes, two pairs blue, one pair brown, the hazel eyes of the redhead so sullen. Why did she look at him with such scorn when he said, "You have all read Chapter 4?" Their silence, their doltish lack of response must entitle him to his little joke. He doubts they have even read Chapter 1, and what can he do if they will not read?

"A test on the first four chapters," he says.

He wishes he could forbid the blond girl to knit; the click of her needles always distracts him, but she is a very tough-looking girl. She has a tough name, the name of a boy. He remembers because the first evening she was listed twice on his roll, as "Gordon Tracy" and "Tracy Gordon," so that now he is uncertain which it is. That first evening, he asked, "There are two?" and then felt a fool, but he had to make sure. There were no men in the class, and surely the office had made a mistake, but American girls sometimes have men's names; there is a woman named Sydney at work.

"I hope you study hard," he says. "I know the work is becoming more difficult but, with application, you will be able to master it, and someday, perhaps, you will work as book-keepers."

The girls are collecting their books. Tracy or Gordon rolls up the green scarf, thrusting her knitting needles through like spears. She says to the Hispanic girl, "We'll see," in a voice that sounds to him ominous. It is the only thing any of the girls have said, and suddenly he is afraid, afraid that none of them will come back. He has frightened them off with talk of a test.

"Wait, please. Let me take attendance. Who is here. You are . . . ?" Rosario, Kathleen, Tracy, Melinda. "Thank you," he says. "Good night."

But not one girl says "Good night" as she leaves. On the hard floor their sneakers squeak as they walk.

Tears come to his eyes. He is so tired. He was up and down all last night with Anil, for Sushila insisted she felt too weak, although he is sure she has only a cold. Mornings, she claims she has nausea and cannot get up to fix the tea, and so it is he who must feed Anil; there are jars in the cupboard of pureed food—applesauce and vegetables—that Anil used to like, but no longer, it seems. The child pushed the spoon away and said, "No!" his body sagging in the high chair, and would not sit up but kept sliding down, evading the spoon, turning his head. Alien flesh, made of food from a jar. At that age, he himself ate real food. He remembers—but he might have been older—remembers being fed by his sister. They are sitting in sunlight on the floor, and Pinky is feeding him *tahiri,* popping the rice and peas into his mouth with her fingers; he wants to do it himself. She is laughing, "What a big boy!" and he reaches for the peas with both hands, the yellow-green peas; he likes them best, wants to pick them out of the rice. But she says, "No, no, only this hand," and holds his hand down. "Only this one."

He blinks back the tears. He won't think of home, of his mother and father, long dead, or of Pinky, with whom he lived until coming here; she would still take him in if he asked. But he won't ask, because of Sushila. Pinky is right: Sushila is spoiled. It comes from being an only child, and it is true she is still very young, but for over two years he has made allowances. When he first brought her here, she did nothing but cry, though he thought she had married him for his green card. Now she wears pants and has learned how to drive and demands to have a car of her own. When he says he wishes her not to wear pants, she says, "Then how am I to keep warm?"

Oh no, life is not as he had hoped.

Tonight he made a fool of himself.

In the ladies' room, Kathleen sprays Wild Musk on her wrists. She gave Bob Wild Musk for Men, not that he uses it. He always smells like the dope he smokes—his clothes, his hair, even his blankets. She can't smoke dope; her mom would smell it, and then she'd say, "All right, lady, move out." And she wants to move out, only she can't. She'd like to move in with Bob. It was a mistake to tell him, though, because that's when he began to chill out. Anyway, she thinks that's when. She asks what's wrong; all he says is "Nothing." But something is—she knows that much. It could be he's met someone else.

She backs on tiptoe into the stall, but the mirror still only shows to her waist. She can't see if her sweater looks grungy down there where it hangs past the knees of her jeans. White—she knew it would be a problem. She climbs up onto the toilet seat. If someone came in, they'd think she was weird. The sweater doesn't look all that bad from a distance. "What're you doing, Kath?" she says. It's not like she plans to go in—she's just going to see if Bob's light is on, going to drive by, she won't even stop. She could creep up to the window and look.

She climbs down. That's sinking too low. If he's got another girlfriend, she'll know soon enough. She looks at the heart she drew last week on the towel dispenser: *Bob + Kath.* Since then, someone has written *Life sucks,* and someone else printed ARE YOU SURE? but you can't tell if the arrow they drew points to *Life sucks* or to her heart. It's better to know if he's cheating on her; it's always better to know. It's like what she copied from over the blackboard: "There is only one good, knowledge, and only one evil, ignorance."

A famous philosopher said that.

Socrates.

Ramesh Mahajan lies awake in the dark, listening to the breathing of his wife. She was asleep when he got home, pretending, perhaps, to be asleep. But now, he thinks, she truly is, and he moves closer, trying to get warm. Her long, thick braid lies between them; he sighs and rolls over on his back. The heater in Anil's room creaks off and on; he turned it down when he came home. Anil had crept out from under his blankets; he sleeps in a garment that resembles a snowsuit.

He must have been too warm, Ramesh thought, but children may simply crawl in their sleep. By now the child may be too cold. Perhaps the heat should have been left where it was. But a man should not have to think of such matters. He swings his legs over the side of the bed—Sushila does not stir—shivers as he steps off the rug, and encounters the icy floor of the hall.

His son lies under slatted shadows thrown by the bars of the crib onto the white blanket, onto the cool cheek. Ramesh slips a finger into the neck of the snowsuit: warm but not too warm. Below, on the lawn: the shadow of the fence, the grass between pickets faintly aglitter and the tops of the parked cars as well, it seems, but without his glasses he cannot be sure.

He had meant to call the landlord. Oh, why is there no one else to keep watch?

In Delhi, it would be daylight now.

Mr. Feldman sings in the basement, his voice floating up each carpeted stair. It's the loneliest singing Kathleen has ever heard; it's making her feel worse and worse.

With her sneaker she nudges the mess on the carpet—dirt and vermiculite, pieces of fern. The clay pot is not broken, but it did crack. Today is an evil day. She knew it was evil the minute she got here; nothing's been right ever since Tuesday. An awful mistake to go over to Bob's, and she never should have knocked on his door. "Oh, it's you, Kath." She can still see his face; he thought she was going to be someone else. "I'd ask you in for a beer, but I've got this heavy-duty test . . ." And meanwhile, he's sort of closing the door as if he thinks she might barge in, and he's doing this sort of shuffle like when is she going to leave? She's so stunned she can't think of a thing to say, and she can hear Bruce inside, real loud.

So she just said, "Forget it."

He never loved her. The least he could've done was tell her. She's going to be stuck at home her whole life, and the only thing she's ever going to do is clean houses.

"I have a friend," Mrs. Feldman began this morning, before Kathleen even got her jacket hung up. "She's a spotless housekeeper, but now it's too much—her husband's just had an operation. I was going to give her your phone number, but I thought I should ask you first."

So what could Kathleen say but "All right"? She didn't even ask if it was an apartment or a house. Never mind that she was thinking of phasing down. She's never going to be a book-keeper, anyhow. Just more and more houses. Mrs. Feldman's friends. Of course, that was before she dropped the fern.

She told herself to be extra careful, like when she was dusting the chandelier, because if anything could go wrong, it would, though she's never broken anything before. She kept waiting to unhook a crystal and have it come zooming down, nicking the table, the finish of which you can see yourself in; it's got about fifty layers of Pledge. But that didn't happen, and when she got around to the windowsill, it was like her mind must have gone somewhere else. She picked up the fern and her wrists went all weak, and now look what she's gone and done.

She didn't need that. She says, "Fucking shit," and she raises her foot and stamps on the pot, which is when Mr. Feldman comes up out of the cellar, and Kathleen can't help it, she bursts into tears. Because he's seen her. At least he heard her. Because she's going to get fired.

She drops to her knees and claws at the dirt, trying to scoop it into the dust rag. The pieces of broken pot are sharp, and she's glad. Maybe her fingers will get cut.

"Is there a tragedy?" Mr. Feldman says. But all she can do is nod. He comes over. "Sweetheart, you'll cut yourself." His hand cups her elbow. "Get up, please."

"I'll buy you another one," Kathleen bawls, but Mr. Feld-man says, "No, no. Please." And he murmurs something under his breath in that language Mrs. Feldman talks to him in. "The plant had lived long enough. It was not a very good plant." He goes and gets her a paper towel. "Come, no more crying." So Kathleen stops. "You go on home. I'll clean this up." But that is too nice. She starts crying again and points to the clock and tries to explain: she hasn't worked her three hours yet. "Not to worry." He pats her shoulder, and then he's leading her toward the door and picking up the money Mrs. Feldman leaves for her under the crystal candy jar. "Don't give it another thought."

He gets her windbreaker out of the closet, tucks the money into the pocket. "You go home and have a nice nap." He opens the door. "We'll see you next week."

So Kathleen walks in a daze to the car. She'll get them some other kind of plant, a Boston fern or a creeping Charlie, or something like a cactus that doesn't drop leaves.

She goes home and has lunch, though it's only eleven, and then gets into bed and sleeps and sleeps. When the little kids come home from school, she takes them to McDonald's for milkshakes. The next day, she studies her bookkeeping. Her mother says she's impressed. Her mother makes everybody quiet down when they're screaming, and she closes the door to the TV room. Also, she answers the phone in case it should be "that wretched Bob." But Bob never calls, though a boy named Jake does.

"I always liked that one," her mother says.

In the closet of Ramesh Mahajan's bedroom is the tissue-paper-wrapped picture of Pinky's holy man that Pinky gave Ramesh when he left home. On Saturday, he unwraps the picture, a photograph of the baba's face: stern, intelligent eyes, gaunt cheeks, wisps of white hair to the collarbone. In Pinky's house there is a shrine with the same photograph and candles and incense. At night, she leaves offerings of food in brass bowls; in the morning, the food is always gone. Rats eat the food, Ramesh fears, but he would never let Pinky suspect.

He gazes into the baba's eyes, which ask, "What right do you have to pray?"

"Baba . . ." Ramesh begins, but agrees: he has no right at

all. He has been negligent, remiss. No wonder things have gone wrong. He sets the picture on Anil's bureau and lights incense and two votive candles, bought last winter when the electricity failed; he had thought it was disconnected. The holy man tells Pinky what to do when she asks. "Baba . . ." Ramesh begins again. And hardly has he uttered the word when the answer comes: Call the landlord.

He does, and the landlord answers—Ramesh doesn't get the answering machine. He says, "It's only 60 degrees in my son's room. Last year it was always at least 68. When will you be able to fix the heat?" And the landlord says, "I'll come take a look," which is much better, much more encouraging a response than Ramesh used to get from the old landlord when the faucets leaked or the sink stopped up, although they never used to have trouble with the heat.

By late afternoon, the apartment is warm, and Sushila is sitting in the living room, watching television, while Anil staggers from doorway to sofa and then back to his father's knee in the kitchen, where Ramesh sits, making up the examination for Tuesday. He makes the questions as simple as possible: multiple choice and blanks to fill in, so that surely all of the girls will pass. But he has a more difficult section as well, about journal entries and financial statements, not too difficult, since the test will be open-book; they can model their answers on the examples in the text. Monday, he'll copy the test at work—thirty copies, just in case.

Sushila comes to the kitchen and says, "It's time for me to feed Anil." She looks very pale and beautiful, even though she is wearing pants. "Would you lift him into the high chair?" she asks, and Ramesh and Anil play a game, Ramesh roaring like a tiger and Anil running as best he can. Which is not at all; he crawls on the floor, with Ramesh laughing and crawling after him.

But on Tuesday there is another access of doubt. What will he do if the girls don't show up? For how long will he need to come to the classroom in the event that a pupil might come back? And will they continue to pay him for teaching if he is merely sitting and waiting?

But it's insulting, Kathleen thinks. She studied so hard, and look at this test. " 'Assets = Liabilities + Capital' is called (a) journalizing, (b) a transaction, (c) the accounting equation." You'd have to be a retard not to pass. You'd have to be a retard to make up the test. Unbelievable. Tracy is right: Mr. Mahajan deserves to be fired. She knows so much more than he's tested her on. She could probably work as a trainee right now. The last part is harder, but not much. She's never coming back to this class.

And neither are Tracy and Rosario. They exchange phone numbers out in the hall. Melinda didn't come tonight. "She had the right idea," Tracy says. They are all going to go on by themselves; they can go a lot faster without Mr. Mahajan. If one of them gets stuck, she can call the other two up. But there's no reason why they might get stuck, except sometimes the book isn't all that clear, like once in a while it leaves out a step, but you can usually figure it out.

Tracy says, "Let's go have a drink. I don't have to rush home tonight."

So the three of them head for the parking lot. As they pass the rest room, Kathleen says, "Wait up." She scrabbles in her purse for her pen and, crossing out *Kath* in the heart, writes *Pepin.*

All three girls have gotten one hundred. He was wrong to despair; they have learned, after all. He's pleased— with them, with himself; their scores speak well for him as a pedagogue. There is only one thing that perplexes him: the red-haired girl, Kathleen, has written something at the bottom of her test, and he doesn't quite understand what it means. "There is only one good, knowledge," it says, "and only one evil, ignorance." At first, he took it as a kind of tribute, but now he isn't so sure. It is one of those sayings of the sort Mary

Mirsky collects—she saves adages from Chinese fortune cookies. On her desk is a sign that says: PERFECT MAY BE THE ENEMY OF GOOD, BUT TRY TO BE PERFECT IN YOUR WORK.

And he does try, he has always tried, but sometimes mistakes will happen. There are worse things than mistakes; almost always they can be rectified. While he proctored the exam, he was reading the timeline and saw that someone had made a mistake. It nearly caused him to laugh out loud, for *Gaul* has been misspelled *Gual.* It looks so queer. How long has it been there, and why did no one ever change it? Students must have stenciled the timeline. Probably no one ever noticed. And so there it is: MEROVINGIAN FRANKS UNDER CLOVIS TAKE CONTROL OF GUAL. Clovis—he doesn't know who that was. But there are worse evils, surely, than ignorance. **Q**

The Clouds of Polonius

Lelia, tragically, is nowhere to be seen.

Her blue sneakers still hang forlornly from the tent pole. It is unclear what we should do, or whether it matters. Grimly, like automata, we call an emergency council; several votes are taken, all inconclusive.

It is the end of a long summer afternoon.

You are fishing, without success, on the northern bend of the river, always a lucky place in times past. The sun has set; the surface of the river is awash with unearthly lights, the phosphorescent harvest of a declining day.

You hear a rustling, as of dead leaves. You turn your head.

Behind you is a strange child.

The dusk has misted his eyebrows with tiny drops of violet dew. You notice, with some concern, that he is wearing a vest.

My old wristwatch has stopped, as if on cue.

I should take it to Mr. D'Alessandro, the jeweler, but I keep putting it off. He makes me nervous. Everything he says sounds like a reproach, or an insult, as if the watch's problems were traceable to some moral failing of mine; as if I had wanted to break it.

Outside, on the front lawn, I hear my sisters playing, their voices like transverse flutes.

I pace back and forth in the great house, which I have entered by stealth—through the cellar—though it is true the front door is never locked.

No one is at home.

In the library, late-afternoon sunlight, shafting uncertainly through the dusty leaded panes.

I gaze nervously about, like a thief.

Far above our heads, on the mountain slope, there are dark skeletal rock formations where they could have hidden her. But we are all too tired to attempt a rescue tonight.

It's more than that: we're tired of Lelia.

Lelia, more than any other member of our expedition— more than the frightful creatures themselves!—is to blame for our exhaustion. We always knew that what appeared to be wind outside the house was in fact history, was time whispering by in its heathery blues; but there was nothing for it, Lelia would have her way, and so it was that we came to the lost valley of the immortals, *her* friends.

You'll never catch anything here, the child says.

You adjust the tension in the reel. Go home, you tell him.

He sits down under a tree.

There seems to be a parent somewhere downstream, beyond the high reeds. *Jeff,* someone calls.

I realize, not without sadness, that I have never seen the upper stories. I begin to explore them, one by one, via stairs that branch toward heaven like the slippery beech in the green-gold yard.

This watch is rusty, says Mr. D'Alessandro, triumphantly. Have you been wearing it in the bathtub?

There is another, much younger man in the shop: Mr. Bertelli. I would prefer to deal with him; but he never speaks.

What's your name? you ask the child.

He does not answer. He is looking vacantly past you, toward the other shore.

In the morning, as we're having breakfast, who should come trooping in but Lelia, surrounded by the creatures.

I study her in amazement. Her bare feet are caked with mud; she smells of spruce gum, or of rain on dry needles.

Please don't stare, Lelia says. You're embarrassing me.

No one speaks for a while. The creatures sit cross-legged on the rocks around the fire, eating gruel.

On the landing, a glance outside: how high I am! Sunset, seemingly, from east and west; the long low rays are reflected in Mrs. Melcher's hundred windows, strafing the fields with brilliant light.

You cast again, then again, out over the dark gray water. Nothing. Time to go; you gather your gear.

All at once you see that the child is crying.

Stop that, you tell him. But he only cries harder.

A long mirror: my sudden reflection.

It must be her room.

An odor of old smoke in the light blue curtains; her bed-clothes, strewn about with adolescent abandon.

You take out your knife, the one with the mother-of-pearl handle, and hold it out in front of you for the child to see.

Now he has grown quiet. After some hesitation, he accepts the gift.

Thank you, he says.

The creatures will not stop talking. It's driving everyone crazy, and it's all Lelia's fault.

Which is more alarming, one of them asks, a ghost or an absence?

Oh, well, says another, if you put it *that* way.

The primordial forms of radiation, says a third, are time and gravity.

Lelia smiles uneasily. One of the creatures is strangely excited; in the center of its forehead is a diamond-shaped patch of skin, perhaps an old cancer, glowing carbuncle-red like the brow of a tiger.

Can you fix it? I ask Mr. D'Alessandro.

No, he says. You'll have to buy a new one.

A few white hairs, carefully arranged to hide his baldness. Mr. Bertelli, like a shadow, saying nothing.

Woolly light of evening sifts down from the high windows.

I slip in between the cold chalky linens, humid like the sea, rotting shroud of a failed Atlantis; I drowse, encircled by camphor and dusty glass.

Downstream, someone has caught a fish.

A goddamn pickerel, says a voice. *All bones and no flesh.*

You peer thoughtfully into the current, as if divining. **Q**

Fairness

The Twaddles are pacing above me, listening, creaking their floors. If the cat meows, they will call Guppie. Alvin Guppie is the landlord, and he knows that my cat is here. The Twaddles don't know that he knows, or that I pay ten dollars a month in cat rent.

When I moved into the building four months ago, Sharon was moving out. She was a night nurse who was between boyfriends. Her old boyfriend had left a fleet of unstripped dining tables in the basement. Her new boyfriend would help her find a buyer. In the meantime, she needed a dry place to keep them and thought of my root cellar, which she still called her root cellar. I helped her drag the tables into the space, the size of a double horse stall, and close the rickety door with two padlocks.

There are four furnaces in the basement, and four root cellars, one for each apartment. Sharon told me that Mr. and Mrs. Twaddle had used her root cellar for two months without her knowing it and had repeatedly taken bulbs from her light socket, so she had had to tell Guppie.

Sharon is a soft white beauty with a musical voice and fluffy hair. Guppie is a family photographer. Guppie told the Twaddles to respect Sharon's privacy or move out.

"Property," I said.

"They've lived in the building for thirty-five years. They think they own the place."

In Kansas, old people I had known did own places and did not steal light bulbs.

"What do they do?" I said.

"He's a retired watchman, and she counts the hours. They pace, loud, as if they want you to hear them."

The day after Sharon moved out, I ran into Mrs. Twaddle in the stairwell. She was going up and I was going down. I held out a hand to her and fudged a smile. Some of my magazines slithered toward the floor.

"You don't belong upstairs," she said.

"I live downstairs," I apologized. "I was looking for a place to put these."

"Storage is in the basement."

Her face was familiar and vicious. Strong dark hair and skin that seemed too bright for her age. I looked away before she did. She had a man's voice.

According to Guppie, the Twaddles have lived in the building for thirty years. He pardons them: "They pay their rent on time and keep the place clean."

"Their floor creaks," I say. That they listen to me is beyond my need to explain.

Bob Opus lives in the apartment across from the Twaddles. We work for the same company and ride the bus together on days when Bob works. Usually he works at night. He keeps mainframes running, even during the holidays.

I plug jargon into sentences. For the technical manuals I write, I need to know how words function in sentences but not necessarily what they mean. Bob is convinced that I speak his language and tells me more than I absorb.

About a month ago, Bob told me that the Twaddles had lived in the building for twenty-five years. Today, while we drink coffee in the cafeteria, I press him for accuracy. He looks insulted, not because I have accused him of lying, I think, but because I care about accuracy.

"Twenty-five or thirty. I don't know. But Sharon exaggerates."

"I still have her tables," I say. "The ones her boyfriend made."

"Boyfriend?"

"The man who lived with her."

He looks punched, and I can tell he is about to say something that will interest me, and that I can stop him if I want to by not seeming interested.

"They're my tables, Doris. I thought she took them." He casts beyond our table. He seems to be looking at the coffee urn. "It's a long story. I don't need to go into it."

When I get home from work in the evenings, I close the curtains and live as quietly as possible. I used to stretch and do sit-ups in the living room, until I discovered a gap in the curtains that even a safety pin wouldn't close. Since the floor creaks, everything I do can be interpreted.

Each of the apartments has a porch and a set of French doors. When the weather turned cold, I covered the doors in heavy plastic. It cured the draft, but the plastic rattles.

One night, I heard someone laughing on my porch. I rolled out of view of all the windows, as if ducking bullets, and lay for a long time on my side, listening to the Twaddles' clock chime upstairs. Their clock plays minor sevenths on the quarter hour. I decided to find a roommate.

Jean Anne sleeps in the back bedroom two nights a week. The rest of the time, she lives with her boyfriend, Jim. They are both beauticians. Guppie has never asked to meet her. He said he doesn't care about roommates, as long as the rent is paid.

Jean Anne posts her rent check on the refrigerator with a bunny magnet. Guppie wants a single payment on the first, so I deposit Jean Anne's check like income. In Kansas, we signed renters' bills of rights that said we were severally liable. Here it's like operating a casino and paying overhead.

The cats are running. The other cat is a stray that Jean Anne adopted. He was starving until she hit him with her car. He is not neutered and croons loudly by my cat's dish. My cat is spayed. Sometimes I am surprised, when rubbing her tummy, to see she still has nipples.

The boy cat canters after her on his wobbly horse legs. The car accident gave him whiplash, so his head is tilted. Lulu lies for him, spayed side up, just as he is about to crash into her. He seems to be looking for a place to smell her.

When Mrs. Twaddle walks past my apartment, she speaks loudly to her husband, whose voice I have never heard. She says, "Beavers!" and "Assholes should learn to shut the door." Then she slams the door in the hallway so hard that the glass quakes.

I am very careful to close that door. When Bob goes out, he slams it for good measure. Outside his door, Mrs. Twaddle yells, "Gopher!"

The woman who lives across the hall from me teaches physics at a parochial school. She leaves the door in the hall-way ajar.

One morning, when I was tired and sleeping in, the buzzer rang. I slipped my jeans on under my nightshirt. A nun was in the hallway.

"Clara?" she said.

"Clara lives in that apartment." I pointed across the hall. Clara opened her door, and the nun disappeared into her dark apartment. Later that night, I heard the nun leave.

"Dykes!" Mrs. Twaddle yelled from the stairwell.

I am trying to decide whether Mrs. Twaddle is an incest survivor or whether she lost a son overseas. I wonder if she drinks vodka. I ask Bob.

"How would I know?" he says.

"Think of the names she calls us—that first time I met her, I bet she thought I had been in your apartment."

"That's because of Sharon."

"What did she have against Sharon?"

"She feared adultery."

"Mr. Twaddle and Sharon?"

"Anyone and Sharon," he says.

I want to tell Bob to forget Sharon, that he is obviously

better off without her, but I don't want to embarrass him by
pointing it out.

"Let's have a party," I say. "Blow off some steam. We can
invite Jean Anne and Jim, you, Clara, me."

"A building party?"

"Anyone you want."

Parties when you are new to town can be like large
flightless birds. Bob invited everyone he could think of,
except Sharon, which seemed to give him pleasure. We decided to have it in my apartment, because my ceilings are
higher.

Bob wears Levi cords to work and Hawaiian shirts to parties. My feeling about parties is that you *can't* overdress. That
goes for small cities, too. I wear a black crepe jumpsuit and
ruby shoes.

Around midnight, I hear a gun go off or a car backfire in
the distance and, minutes later, loud banging on my back
door. I find Bob and turn down the music, thinking it is the
Twaddles coming to complain. No one is there. But there is
a bowl on the doorstep with something red in it.

"Entrails," Bob says, sniffing it.

"Entrails?" Then it hits me. I run inside, sure that Lulu
slipped out when the guests arrived. Bob runs after me.

"Doris, wait. It's one of Sharon's bowls."

I crawl on the floor and look under the sofa. "Bob, everyone has Pyrex. I have a bowl like that."

I stand up on the sofa. I normally cannot make announce-
ments, but I tell them, too loudly perhaps, that they must
search my apartment and not go outside.

Jean Anne keeps calm and resourceful. She describes
Lulu's markings to people in the living room. I go to the
kitchen and run the electric can opener. The boy cat shoots out
of hiding like a spark.

"I'll feed him," Jean Anne says. "He must be hungry."

ANN BOGLE

Parties end the minute the hostess has a personal crisis.

" 'Bye, Bob," they are all suddenly saying. " 'Bye, Doris, hope she turns up. If I were you, I'd go up there."

I just look at my shoes. New shoes have the power to make you feel happy when nothing else will.

"Where is everyone going?" Jean Anne says, holding the cat-food spoon.

Bob rummages in my cupboards. "Doris, there's no bowl like that in here. Are you sure you have one?"

"I did," I say vaguely. "I thought."

I leave the apartment and trudge upstairs, numb and unafraid. Mr. Twaddle answers the door. Mrs. Twaddle peers over his shoulder. They are in bathrobes and have the stunned gaze of sleepers.

"My cat," I say.

"Do you know what time it is, miss?"

"No, but you should," I say, thinking of her clock. "My cat is missing, probably dead, and you have a thing for animals."

"You'll hear from Alvin Guppie in the morning, sister." She stands back, but Mr. stays firm.

"I hope you find him."

"Henry, shut the door."

When I get back to my apartment, Jean Anne and Jim are picking up beer cans.

"Oh well," Jim says. "It was fun while it lasted."

"What are you going to do now?" Jean Anne says.

I squat on the floor and decide not to cry. A blister has formed at the back of my ankle, and for a moment, I think that this is the problem.

Jean Anne steps over me and answers the door. "Doris," she says, "look who's home."

"She climbed in bed with me," Clara says, setting Lulu down. "I didn't even know what it was."

Bob is still in the kitchen repeating how sick Sharon is. "Practical joker," Jim says. "That's who did it."

I chew on the word "practical." Lulu passes under my legs. I try to imagine what she thinks about it. She kicks her leg behind her ear and bites hard on her ankle.

The Twaddles are pacing upstairs. Their floors are creaking. They are yelling something.

It is impossible to make out the words. **Q**

Manqué

I cartwheeled out of the throat of the thing, like a caricature bending up into a cloud hovering beneath the roof-beams. The fabric of it was slick, and when it caught the light, shone back peach-colored. Lace-framed and flushed, I walked into the orange woodlight. So then a spire rises like pressed palms and in the clinging hook and line of touch, fronds serrate the empty clouds. The lawn is a continent in the gardener's palm.

I cut the pew-stained air, a pendulum naked as cherries. Oh, I am coy, but what of this. The empty dress walks onward. What do I want from these moments, oh, I suppose, and yet am I to expect this poverty of ribbons? Bent upward in the air away from a tide of fingers. A miracle of fleshes passing up through the voices like smoke that turns the very thought of skinsongs gray.

And then a him? Please, must I contemplate a him? No, as I said, I slip up through the frill collar and out into the air, where only the Sacrament and I dwell in brittle silence. Bless these spindly limbs and let their naked gray shadows hold hard the drab and greensour piety of paraffin and crossed sticks. Nailed upon the heavy smell of owlwives, sweaty legs and sooty petticoats curling like bent wires in his mouth.

God bless the dust in the shaft of light, for in it curls a young girl's eyelashes. Wear this thing! I won't, I say. As if the Virgin were a clown. As if the throat of a bird were merely a finger for a ring. As if things forked and grew in the ditches of the aisle.

I am curled up, I tell you, away, lifted. The censer turns my bare breasts the color of ash. The empty dress walks on toward what? All this merely the fabric passing over my face.

But there is no seam in my imaginings. My head pops out through the collar and into the light, and the rest remains strapped in place. Your faces dimple and giggle. They press together, cheek to cheek, like the sides of a coal chute. I slip on them down to this silly idea of a him. **Q**

Ralph the Duck

I woke up at 5:25 because the dog was vomiting. I carried seventy-five pounds of heaving golden retriever to the door and poured him onto the silver, moonlit snow. "Good boy," I said, because he'd done his only trick. Outside, he retched, and I went back up, passing the sofa on which Fanny lay. I tiptoed with enough weight on my toes to let her know how considerate I was while she was deserting me. She blinked her eyes. I swear I heard her blink her eyes. Whenever I tell her that I hear her blink her eyes, she tells me I'm lying; but I can hear the damp slap of lash after I have made her weep.

In bed and warm again, noting the red digital numbers (5:29) and certain that I wouldn't sleep, I didn't. I read a book about men who kill each other for pay or for their honor. I forget which, and so did they. It was 5:45, the alarm would buzz at 6:00, and I would make a pot of coffee and start the woodstove; I would call Fanny and pour her coffee into her mug; I would apologize, because I always did, and then she would forgive me if I hadn't been too awful—I didn't think I'd been that bad—and we would stagger through the day, exhausted but pretty sure we were all right, and we'd sleep that night, probably after sex, and then we'd waken in the same bed to the alarm at 6:00, or the dog, if he'd returned to the frozen deer carcass he'd been eating in the forest on our land. He loved what made him sick. The alarm went off, I got into jeans and woolen socks and a sweatshirt, and I went downstairs to let the dog in. He'd be hungry, of course.

I was the oldest college student in America, I thought. But of course I wasn't. There were always ancient women with parchment for skin who graduated at seventy-nine from places like Barnard and the University of Georgia. I was only forty-two, and I hardly qualified as a student. I patrolled the college at night in a Bronco with a leaky exhaust system, and I went from room to room in the classroom buildings, kicking out students who were studying or humping in chairs—they'd do it *anywhere*—and answering emergency calls with my little blue light winking on top of the truck. I didn't carry a gun or a billy, but I had a flashlight that took six batteries and I'd used it twice on some of my overprivileged Northeastern playboy part-time classmates. On Tuesdays and Thursdays, I would waken at 6:00 with my wife, and I'd do my homework, and work around the house, and go to school at 11:30 to sit there for an hour and a half while thirty-five stomachs growled with hunger and boredom and this guy gave instruction about books. Because I was on the staff, the college let me take a course for nothing every term. I was getting educated, in a kind of slow-motion way—it would take me something like fifteen or sixteen years to graduate, and I would no doubt get an F in gym and have to repeat—and there were times when I respected myself for it. Fanny often did, and that was fair incentive.

I am not unintelligent. *You are not an unintelligent writer,* my professor wrote on my paper about Nathaniel Hawthorne. We had to read short stories, I and the other students, and then we had to write little essays about them. I told how I saw Kafka and Hawthorne in a similar light, and I was not unintelligent, he said. He ran into me at dusk one time, when I answered a call about a dead battery and found out it was him. I jumped his Buick from the Bronco's battery, and he was looking me over, I could tell, while I clamped onto the terminals and cranked it up. He was a tall, handsome guy who never wore a suit. He wore khakis and sweaters, loafers or sneaks, and he was always talking to the female students with the brightest hair and best builds. But he couldn't get a Buick going on an ice-cold night, and he didn't know enough to look for cells starting to go bad. I told him he would probably have to get a new battery, and he looked me over the way men sometimes do with other men who fix their cars for them.

"Vietnam?"

I said, "Too old."

"Not at the beginning. Not if you were an advisor. So-called. Or one of the Phoenix Project fellas?"

I was wearing a watch cap made of navy wool and an old Marine fatigue jacket. Slick characters on the order of my professor like it if you're a killer, or at least a one-time middle-weight fighter. I smiled like I knew something. "Take it easy," I said, and I went back to the truck to swing around the cemetery at the top of the campus. They'd been known to screw in down-filled sleeping bags on horizontal stones up there, and the dean of students didn't want anybody dying of frostbite while joined at the hip to a matriculating fellow resident of our Northeastern camp for the overindulged.

He blinked his high beams at me as I went.

"You are not an unintelligent driver," I said.

Fanny had left me a bowl of something made with sausages and sauerkraut and potatoes, and the dog hadn't eaten too much more than his fair share. He watched me eat his leftovers and then make myself a king-sized drink composed of sourmash whiskey and ice. In our back room, which is on the northern end of the house, and cold for sitting in that close to dawn, I sat and watched the texture of the sky change. It was going to snow, and I wanted to see the storm come up the valley. I woke up that way, sitting in the rocker with its loose right arm, holding a watery drink and thinking right away of the girl I'd convinced to go back inside. She'd been standing outside her dormitory, looking up at a window that was dark in the midst of all those lighted panes—they never turned a light off and often let the faucets run half the night—and crying onto her bathrobe. She was barefoot in shoepacs, the brown ones so many of them wore unlaced, and for all I know, she was naked under the robe. She was beautiful, I thought, and she was somebody's redheaded daughter, standing in a quadrangle how many miles from home and weeping.

"He doesn't love anyone," the kid told me. "He doesn't `

love his wife—I mean his ex-wife. And he doesn't love the ex-wife before that, or the one before that. And you know what? He doesn't love me. I don't know anyone who *does*!"

"It isn't your fault if he isn't smart enough to love you," I said, steering her toward the truck.

She stopped. She turned. "You know him?"

I couldn't help it. I hugged her hard, and she let me, and then she stepped back, and of course I let her go. "Don't you *touch* me! Is this sexual harassment? Do you know the rules? Isn't this sexual harassment?"

"I'm sorry," I said at the door to the truck. "But I think I have to be able to give you a grade before it counts as harassment."

She got in. I told her we were driving to the dean of students' house. She smelled like marijuana and something very sweet, maybe one of those coffee-with-cream liqueurs you don't buy unless you hate to drink.

As the heat of the truck struck her, she started going kind of clay-gray-green, and I reached across her to open the window.

"You touched my breast!" she said.

"It's the smallest one I've touched all night, I'm afraid."

She leaned out the window and gave her rendition of my dog.

But in my rocker, waking up, at whatever time in the morning in my silent house, I thought of her as someone's child. Which made me think of ours, of course. I went for more ice, and I started on a wet breakfast. At the door of the dean of students' house, she'd turned her chalky face to me and asked, "What grade would you give me, then?"

It was a week composed of two teachers locked out of their offices late at night, a Toyota with a flat and no spare, an attempted rape on a senior girl walking home from the library, a major fight outside a fraternity house (broken wrist and significant concussion), and variations on breaking-and-entering. I was scolded by the director of nonacademic services for embracing a student who was drunk; I told him to keep his job, but he called me back because I was right to hug her, he said, and also wrong, but what the hell, and he'd promised to admonish me, and now he had, and would I please stay. I thought of the fringe benefits—graduation in only sixteen years—so I went back to work.

My professor assigned a story called "A Rose for Emily," and I wrote him a paper about the mechanics of corpse-fucking, and how, since she clearly couldn't screw her dead boyfriend, she was keeping his rotten body in bed because she truly loved him. I called the paper "True Love." He gave me a B and wrote *See me, pls.* In his office after class, his feet up on his desk, he trimmed a cigar with a giant folding knife he kept in his drawer.

"You've got to clean the hole out," he said, "or they don't draw."

"I don't smoke," I said.

"Bad habit. Real *habit,* though. I started in smoking 'em in Georgia, in the service. My CO smoked 'em. We collaborated on a brothel inspection one time, and we ended up smoking these with a couple of women—" He waggled his eyebrows at me, now that his malehood had been established.

"Were the women smoking them, too?"

He snorted laughter through his nose, while the greasy smoke came curling off his thin, dry lips. "They were pretty smoky, I'll tell ya!" Then he propped up his feet—he was wearing cowboy boots that day—and he sat forward. "It's a little hard to explain. But—hell. You just don't say *fuck* when you write an essay for a college prof. Okay?" Like a scoutmaster with a kid he'd caught in the outhouse jerking off: "All right? You don't wanna do that."

"Did it shock you?"

"Fuck, no, it didn't shock me. I just told you. It violates certain proprieties."

"But if I'm writing it to you, like a letter—"

"You're writing it for posterity. For some mythical reader someplace, not just me. You're making a *statement.*"

"Right. My statement said how hard it must be for a woman to fuck with a corpse."

"And a point worth making. I said so. Here."

"But you said I shouldn't say it."

"No. Listen. Just because you're talking about fucking, you don't have to say *fuck*. Does that make it any clearer?"

"No."

"I wish you'd lied to me just now," he said.

I nodded. I did, too.

"Where'd you do your service?" he asked.

"Baltimore. Baltimore, Maryland."

"What's in Baltimore?"

"Railroads. I worked with freight runs of army matériel. I killed a couple of bums on the rod with my bare hands, though."

He snorted again, but I could see how disappointed he was. He'd been banking on my having been a murderer. Interesting guy in one of my classes, he must have told some terrific woman at an overpriced meal: I just *know* the guy was a rubout specialist in 'Nam, he had to have said. I figured I should come to work wearing my fatigue jacket and a red bandanna tied around my head, say "man" to him a couple of times, hang a fist in the air for grief and solidarity, and look terribly worn, exhausted by experiences he was fairly certain that he envied me. His dungarees were ironed, I noticed.

On Saturday, we went back to the campus, because Fanny wanted to see a movie called *The Seven Samurai.* I fell asleep, and I'm afraid I snored. She let me sleep until the auditorium was almost empty. Then she kissed me awake. "Who was screaming in my dream?" I asked her.

"Kurosawa," she said.

"Who?"

"Ask your professor friend."

I looked around, but he wasn't there. "Not an unweird man," I said.

We went home and cleaned up after the dog and put him out. We drank a little Spanish brandy and went upstairs and made love. I was fairly premature, you might say, but one way and another, by the time we fell asleep, we were glad to be there with each other, and glad that it was Sunday coming up the valley toward us, and nobody with it. The dog was howling at another dog someplace, or at the moon, or maybe just at his moon-thrown shadow on the snow. I did not strangle him when I opened the back door, and he limped happily past me and stumbled up the stairs. I followed him into our bedroom and groaned for just being satisfied as I got into bed.

You'll notice I didn't say fuck.

He stopped me in the hall after class on a Thursday and asked me, How's it goin'?—just one of the kickers drinking sour beer and eating pickled eggs and watching the tube in a country bar. How's it goin'? I nodded. I wanted a grade from the man, and I did want to learn about expressing myself. I nodded and made what I thought was a smile. He'd let his mustache grow out and his hair grow longer. He was starting to wear dark shirts with lighter ties. I thought he looked like someone in *The Godfather.* He still wore those light little loafers or his high-heeled cowboy boots. His corduroy pants looked baggy. I guess he wanted them to look that way. He motioned me to the wall of the hallway, and he looked up and said, "How about the Baltimore stuff?"

I said, "Yeah?"

"Was that really true?" He was almost blinking, he wanted so much for me to be a damaged war vet just looking for a tower to climb into and start firing from. The college didn't have a tower you could get up into, though I'd once spent an ugly hour chasing a drunken ATO down from the roof of the observatory. "You were just clocking through boxcars in Baltimore?"

123

I said, "Nah."

"I thought so!" He gave a kind of sigh.

"I killed people," I said.

"You know, I could have sworn you did," he said.

I nodded, and he nodded back.

I'd made him so happy.

The assignment was to write something to influence somebody. He called it Rhetoric and Persuasion. We read an essay by George Orwell and "A Modest Proposal" by Jonathan Swift. I liked the Orwell better, but I wasn't comfortable with it. He talked about "niggers," and I felt him saying it two ways.

I wrote *Ralph the Duck*.

Once upon a time, there was a duck named Ralph who didn't have any feathers on either wing. So when the cold wind blew, Ralph said, Brr, and shivered and shook.

What's the matter? Ralph's mommy asked.

I'm *cold*, Ralph said.

Oh, the mommy said. Here. I'll keep you warm.

So she spread her big, feathery wings and hugged Ralph tight, and when the cold wind blew, Ralph was warm and snuggly, and fell fast asleep.

The next Thursday, he was wearing canvas pants and hiking boots. He mentioned kind of casually to some of the girls in the class how whenever there was a storm he wore his Lake District walking outfit. He had a big, hairy sweater on. I kept waiting for him to make a noise like a mountain goat. But the girls seemed to like it. His boots made a creaky squeak on the linoleum of the hall when he caught up with me after class.

"As I told you," he said, "it isn't unappealing. It's just— not a college theme."

"Right," I said. "Okay. You want me to do it over?"

"No," he said. "Not at all. But the D will remain your grade. I'll read something else if you want to write it."

"This'll be fine," I said.

"Did you understand the assignment?"

"Write something to influence someone—Rhetoric and Persuasion."

We were at his office door and the redheaded kid who had gotten sick in my truck was waiting for him. She looked at me like one of us was in the wrong place, which struck me as accurate enough. He was interested in getting into his office with the redhead, but he remembered to turn around and flash me a grin he seemed to think he was known for.

Instead of going on shift a few hours after class, the way I'm supposed to, I told my supervisor I was sick, and I went home. Fanny was frightened when I came in, because I don't get sick and I don't miss work. She looked at my face and she grew sad. I kissed her hello and went upstairs, to change. I always used to change my clothes when I was a kid as soon as I came home from school. I put on jeans and a flannel shirt and thick wool socks, and I made myself a dark drink of sourmash. Fanny poured herself some wine and came into the cold northern room a few minutes later. I was sitting in the rocker, looking over the valley. The wind was lining up a lot of rows of cloud, so that the sky looked like a baked trout when you lift the skin off. "It'll snow," I said to her.

She sat on the old sofa and waited. After a while, she said, "I wonder why they always call it a mackerel sky."

"Good eating, mackerel," I said.

Fanny said, "Shit! You're never that laconic unless you feel crazy. What's wrong? Who'd you punch out at the playground?"

"We had to write a composition," I said.

"Did he like it?"

"He gave me a D."

"Well, you're familiar enough with D's. I never saw you get this low over a grade."

"I wrote about Ralph the duck."

She said, "You did?" She said, "Baby." She came over and

stood beside the rocker and leaned into me and hugged my head and neck. "Baby," she said. "Baby."

It was the worst of the winter's storms, and one of the worst in years. That afternoon they closed the college, which they almost never do. But the roads were jammed with snow over ice, and now it was freezing rain on top of that, and the only people working at the school that night were the operator who took emergency calls and me. Everyone else had gone home except the students, and most of them were inside. The ones who weren't were drunk, and I kept on sending them in and telling them to act like grownups. A number of them said they were, and I really couldn't argue. I had the bright beams on, the defroster set high, the little blue light winking, and a thermos of sourmash and hot coffee that I sipped from every time I had to get out of the truck or every time I realized how cold all that wetness was out there.

About eight o'clock, as the rain was turning back to snow and the cold was worse, the roads impossible, just as I was done helping a county sander on the edge of the campus pull a panel truck out of a snowbank, I got an emergency call from the college operator. We had a student missing. The room-mates thought the kid was headed for the quarry. This meant I had to get the Bronco up on a narrow road above the campus, above the old cemetery, into all kinds of woods and rough track that I figured would be choked with ice and snow. Any kid up there would really have to want to be there, and I couldn't go in on foot, because you'd only want to be there on account of drugs, booze, or craziness, and either way I'd be needing blankets and heat, and then a fast ride down to the hospital in town. So I dropped into four-wheel drive to get me up the hill above the campus, bucking snow and sliding on ice, putting all the heater's warmth up onto the windshield, be-cause I couldn't see much more than swarming snow. My feet were still cold from the tow job, and it didn't seem to matter that I had on heavy socks and insulated boots I'd coated with waterproofing. I shivered, and I thought of Ralph the duck.

I had to grind the rest of the way from the cemetery in four-wheel low, and in spite of the cold, I was smoking my gearbox by the time I was close enough to the quarry—they really did take a lot of the rocks for the campus buildings from there—to see I'd have to make my way on foot to where she was. It was a kind of scooped-out shape, maybe four or five stories high, where she stood—well, wobbled is more like it. She was as chalky as she'd been the last time, and her red hair didn't catch the light anymore. It just lay on her like something that had died on top of her head. She was in a white nightgown that was plastered to her body. She had her arms crossed as if she wanted to be warm. She swayed, kind of, in front of the big, dark, scooped-out rockface, where the trees and brush had been cleared for trucks and earthmovers. She looked tiny against all the darkness. From where I stood, I could see the snow driving down in front of the lights I'd left on, but I couldn't see it near her. All it looked like around her was dark. She was shaking with the cold, and she was crying.

I had a blanket with me, and I shoved it down the front of my coat to keep it dry for her, and because I was so cold. I waved. I stood in the lights and I waved. I don't know what she saw—a big shadow, maybe. I surely didn't reassure her, because when she saw me she backed up, until she was near the face of the quarry. She couldn't go any farther, anyway.

I called, "Hello! I brought a blanket. Are you cold? I thought you might want a blanket."

Her roommates had told the operator about pills, so I didn't bring her the coffee laced with mash. I figured I didn't have all that much time, anyway, to get her down and pumped out. The booze with whatever pills she'd taken would make her die that much faster.

I hated that word. Die. It made me furious with her. I heard myself seething when I breathed. I pulled my scarf and collar up above my mouth. I didn't want her to see how close I might come to wanting to kill her because she wanted to die.

I called, "Remember me?"

I was closer now. I could see the purple mottling of her skin. I didn't know if it was cold or dying. It probably didn't matter much to distinguish between them right now, I thought. That made me smile. I felt the smile, and I pulled the scarf down so she could look at it. She didn't seem awfully reassured.

"You're the sexual harassment guy," she said. She said it very slowly. Her lips were clumsy. It was like looking at a ventriloquist's dummy.

"I gave you an A," I said.

"When?"

"It's a joke," I said. "You don't want me making jokes. You want me to give you a nice warm blanket, though. And then you want me to take you home."

She leaned against the rockface when I approached. I pulled the blanket out, then zipped my jacket back up. The snow had stopped, I realized, and that wasn't really a very good sign. It felt as if an arctic cold was descending in its place. I held the blanket out to her, but she only looked at it.

"You'll just have to turn me in," I said. "I'm gonna hug you again."

She screamed, "No more! I don't want any more hugs!"

But she kept her arms on her chest, and I wrapped the blanket around her and stuffed a piece into each of her tight, small fists. I didn't know what to do for her feet. Finally, I got down on my haunches in front of her. She crouched down, too, protecting herself.

"No," I said. "No. You're fine."

I took off the woolen mittens I'd been wearing. Mittens keep you warmer than gloves because they trap your hand's heat around the fingers and palms at once. Fanny had knitted them for me. I put a mitten as far onto each of her feet as I could. She let me. She was going to collapse, I thought.

"Now let's go home," I said. "Let's get you better."

With her funny, stiff lips, she said, "I've been very self-indulgent and weird, and I'm sorry. But I'd really like to die." She sounded so reasonable that I found myself nodding in agreement as she spoke.

"You can't just die," I said.

"Aren't I dying already? I took all of them, and then"—she giggled like a child, which of course is what she was—"I borrowed different ones from other people's rooms. See, this isn't some teenage cry like for *help*. Understand? I'm seriously interested in death and I have to like stay out here a little longer and fall asleep. All right?"

"You can't do that," I said. "You ever hear of Vietnam?"

"I saw that movie," she said. "With the opera in it? *Apocalypse?* Whatever."

"I was there!" I said. "I killed people! I helped to kill them! And when they die, you see their bones later on. You dream about their bones and blood on the ends of the splintered ones, and this kind of mucous stuff coming out of their eyes. You probably heard of guys having dreams like that, didn't you? Whacked-out Vietnam vets? That's me, see? So I'm telling you, I know about dead people and their eyeballs and everything falling out. And people keep dreaming about the dead people they knew, see? You can't make people dream about you like that! It isn't fair!"

"You dream about me?" She was ready to go. She was ready to fall down, and I was going to lift her up and get her to the truck.

"I will," I said. "If you die."

"I want you to," she said. Her lips were hardly moving now. Her eyes were closed. "I want you all to."

I dropped my shoulder and put it into her waist and picked her up and carried her down to the Bronco. She was talking, but not a lot, and her voice leaked down my back. I jammed her into the truck and wrapped the blanket around her better and then put another one down around her feet. I strapped her in with the seat belt. She was shaking, and her eyes were closed and her mouth open. She was breathing. I checked that twice, once when I strapped her in and then again when I strapped myself in and backed up hard into a sapling and took it down. I got us into first gear, held the clutch in, leaned over to listen for breathing, heard it—shallow panting, like a kid asleep on your lap for a nap—and then I put the gear in and howled down the hillside on what I thought might be the road.

We passed the cemetery. I told her that was a good sign. She didn't respond. I found myself panting, too, as if we were breathing for each other. It made me dizzy, but I couldn't stop. We passed the highest dorm, and I dropped the truck into four-wheel high. The cab smelled like burned oil and hot metal. We were past the chapel now, and the observatory, the president's house, then the bookstore. I had the blue light winking and the V-6 roaring, and I drove on the edge of out-of-control, sensing the skids just before I slid into them and getting back out of them as I needed to. I took a little fender off once, and a bit of the corner of a classroom building, but I worked us back on-course, and all I needed to do now was negotiate the sharp turn around the Administration Building, past the library, then floor it for the straight run to the town's main street and then the hospital.

I was panting into the mike, and the operator kept saying, "Say again?"

I made myself slow down some, and I said we'd need stomach pumping, and to get the names of the pills from her friends in the dorm, and I'd be there in less than five minutes or we were crumpled up someplace and dead.

"Roger," the radio said. "Roger all that."

My throat tightened and tears came into my eyes. They were helping us, they'd told me: Roger.

I said to the girl, whose head was slumped and whose face looked too blue all through its whiteness, "You know, I had a girl once. My wife, Fanny. She and I had a small girl one time."

I reached over and touched her cheek.

It was cold.

The truck swerved, and I got my hands on the wheel.

I came to the campus gates doing fifty on the ice and snow, smoking the engine, grinding the clutch, and I bounced off a wrought-iron fence to give me the curve going left that I needed. On a pool table, it would have been a bank shot worth applause. The town cop picked me up and got out ahead of me and let the street have all the lights and noise it could want. We banged up to the emergency-room entrance and I was out and at the other door before the cop on duty, Elmo St. John, could loosen his seat belt. I loosened hers, and I carried her into the lobby of the ER. They had a gurney, and doctors, and they took her away from me. I tried to talk to them, but they made me sit down and do my shaking on a dirty sofa decorated with drawings of little spinning wheels. Somebody brought me hot coffee, I think it was Elmo, but I couldn't hold it.

"They won't," he kept saying to me. "They won't."

"What?"

"You just been sitting there for a minute and a half like St. Vitus dancing, telling me, 'Don't let her die. Don't let her die.' "

"Oh."

"You all *right*?"

"How about the kid?"

"They'll tell us soon."

"She better be all right."

"That's right."

"She—somebody's gonna have to tell me plenty if she isn't."

"That's right."

"She better not die this time," I guess I said.

Fanny came downstairs to see where I was. I was at the northern windows, looking through the mullions down the valley to the faint red line along the mounds and little peaks of the ridge beyond the valley. The sun was going to come up, and I was looking for it.

Fanny stood behind me. I could hear her. I could smell her hair and the sleep on her. The crimson line widened, and I squinted at it. I heard the dog limp in behind her, catching up. He panted and I knew why his panting sounded familiar. She put her hands on my shoulders and arms. I made muscles to impress her with, and then I let them go, and let my head drop down until my chin was on my chest.

"I didn't think you'd be able to sleep after that," Fanny said.

"I brought enough adrenaline home to run a football team."

"But you hate being a hero, huh? You're hiding in here because somebody's going to call, or come over, and want to talk to you—her parents for shooting sure, sooner or later. Or is that supposed to be part of the service up at the playground? Saving their suicidal daughters. Almost dying to find them in the woods and driving too fast for *any* weather, much less what we had last night. Getting their babies home. The bastards." She was crying. I knew she was going to be. I could hear the soft sound of her lashes. She sniffed, and I could feel her arm move as she felt for the tissues on the coffee table.

"I have them over here," I said. "On the windowsill."

"Yes." She blew her nose, and the dog thumped his tail. He seemed to think it one of Fanny's finer tricks, and he had wagged for her for thirteen years whenever she'd done it. "Well, you're going to have to talk to them," she said.

"I will," I said. "I will." The sun was in our sky now, climbing. We had built the room so we could watch it climb. "I think that jackass with the smile, my prof? She showed up a lot at his office the last few weeks. He called her 'my advisee,' you know? The way those guys sound about what they're achieving by getting up and shaving and going to work and saying the same thing every day. Every year. Well, she was his advisee, I bet. He was shoving home the old advice."

"She'll be okay," Fanny said. "Her parents will take her home and love her up and get her some help." Fanny began to cry again, then she stopped. She blew her nose, and the dog's tail thumped. She kept a hand between my shoulder and my neck. "So tell me what you'll tell a waiting world. How'd you talk her out?"

"Well, I didn't, really. I got up close and picked her up and carried her, is all."

"You didn't say *any*thing?"

"Sure, I did. Kid's standing in the snow outside of a lot of pills, you're gonna say something."

"So what'd you *say*?"

"I told her stories," I said. "I did Rhetoric and Persuasion."

Fanny said, "Go in early on Thursday, you go in half an hour early, you get that guy to jack up your grade." **Q**

The old man's nose bleeds

Loading Pumpkins

Middle fall and heartbreak weather:
The fog burns off to dusklight by 10 A.M.
We are paid by the truckload,
after hacking the shocked and coddled stems,
an easy string of tosses into the ride north.

It is strange to harvest
fruit that no one will eat,
as some light is stranger than darkness:
ignis fatuus, St. Elmo's fire,
the jack-o'-lantern in whose service
we now pile the mild and featureless heads.

Think of it as Adam's revenge,
this butchery of untasted fruit.
We work and pass along the orange weight
by a harbor discovered
by a lost and wondering English pirate.

It is autumn at Half Moon Bay,
and we know only what we have to.
We plant what fruit we can
for whatever purpose it may eventually serve,
hold high our carved, strange, and eviscerated
    lanterns,
guard tenderly all the way north
our stolen cargo of seed, guts, and, someday, light.

The Spy

At 44th and Vanderbilt,
across the street from Grand Central Station,
the British caught Nathan Hale (Yale,
Class of '73), his pockets full
of notes and nonchalance.

It was more like a suburb then;
you would think he'd have made up something,
some errand in Haarlem, or brats to instruct
in New Haven, anything to lose him
among war's innumerable passers-through,
but no, he found jeopardy a better fit
than the spy's gray-stained suit of fog,
and his lips suddenly burned with common sense
and the rights of man, while his jailers
nodded in sympathy, pursed their lips,
urged him to go on, listened all night.
Naturally, they hanged him the next morning.

I always wind up wondering about
the weather on famous days.
That was in late September, as it is now,
and today is a cold dither of wind
and leaves and dust as I read his plaque.

Perhaps he never even noticed.
I am no longer young and he was twenty-one
when they scratched his neck
with East India Company jute.
He was twenty-one and schoolmaster to the end,

trying to think of something the kids would
    memorize,
but I am the better spy, and have learned
that there is no one, none,
who does not regret that he has but one life to
    lose.

The Raccoon

It killed my dog.
The screams seemed careful,
a visit of obligation.
My barefoot steps suddenly mulled
in hot copper blood.
The dog hadn't died yet,
but I could feel her packing.

I remember a picture from the South
of one treed, its face lanced
by flashlight, and one paw
batting off the air
breathed from the wheezing hounds.

The killers among us have a weight problem.
They wash their hands.
Frequently, they embark on show business careers.
The killers prefer to think of themselves
as curious, prying open the can,
pursuing their vocations of salvage and rescue.

There will be a time,
perhaps as you're sipping soup
alone in your kitchen, when, summoned,
you will look up. And there,
through the backyard window:

small hands on the glass,
a face, a ragged strip of night.

Horseback, Prospect Park

All this soft rocking and liquid perception
has its effect: even when the horse
routinely stumbles, it is a ship's roll,
a lateral swim.

And the park, from this brief height,
offers a different instruction: the leaves
are now understood as they understand themselves.
We walk through the complexion of autumn,
shadow and beam, until we come
to Prospect Lake, dredged, new, nearly Caribbean,
while a vagrant sun dawdles,
skipping its stones across the surface.

It will be as though this never happened.
The teeth of my grazing horse will grind on and
        on;
the lake will cloud to the color of disappointment.
The solid world will hold my hand
in a landscape endless as thought.

The Last Day

This is how the end will come.
You will be walking by an ocean
with the sun riding alongside.
An old woman will be walking
a small brown dog.
She will stop, lean over,
ask the dog again and again:
What do you want?
What is it that you want?

Above you, the black Percheron
will begin its slow stepping,
carrying all night and against all purpose
its saddleful of stars.

The Boys I Hit in the Face

Every one of them, his red oval reshaped
by my own hand, retains his alphabetical place:
Frankie Casabonne, John Robbins,
even Michael Smith, with his one bad eye,
bland and decent as his name,
opens an occasional door in my brain,
looks in, finds a mirror, tries to be quiet
as he shuts the room again.

But the boys who hit me—they are all gone;
I cannot recall any of them.
I wonder, though, if I live on in them,
if that twist of rage around my mouth
nests itself in their helices,
if that braid of pain will never be cropped.

Now the truth: I was, for all that,
a coward. The blood was one thing,
but the face something else entirely,
the uncomprehending eye squeezed tight shut,
the understanding that this was real trouble,
and I, knowing I had performed this,
I had changed a face to this terrible privacy,
became frightened and held back my hand
from the victory blow, the business unfinished,
my friends shouting and confused.

But the blood was not it.
There was even something good about that,

flying across my arm, a dik-dik jumping to a
    brilliance
removed from the body's familiar shade,
looking back on the face and its plodding tears,
then plunging on, up and out
from its old, half-known, utterly vanished life.

Hey, Schliemann

Hey, Schliemann, you wanna find me?

I'm under a granite stone—
eight digits, a dash, and cliché.
You wanna know me?
I'm wearing a gold ring,
a suit, and cardboard shoes.

Schliemann, dig me up; you
found Troy, guess my religion.

I'm the type of my time.
. . . A certain type of my time.
Look at my spine,
I never worked.

Schliemann, dig up my house;
yes, it centered around the shower.

Yes, I wander about at night
with my beer in a plastic jug
to fool the Baptists.

Aphorisms

Some rhythms can't stand
the imposition of words,
the Cadillac that's meaning
busting the bridge.

Do you really want me
to say something
out of our wasted fondling?
A long harvest for a little corn.

Further Diversions

I never lost the thrill of scattering
pink poison among the thick fists
of hog manure. Waves of flies circled,

gathered, rubbed their hands and
feet, filled up, got drunk, fell over,

crinkling into stillness. Everywhere.
Everywhere was another frame in the
process, a separate photo of the

progression, new ones pulling through
the black, piled corpses for a chance.

Up North

We'll have breakfast.
We'll have breakfast in the grass.
It'll be nearly as pleasant
as the coffee under the trees.

Some will sit in the sun,
some in the shade, but we'll
all look up at the airplanes.

The wings make patterns
on the sun-tea jar.

Mouy Gie

Oh, mouy Gauwd,
Oi've gauwt
tha woist gie
in tha woild.
Neva duz he
send me flouwas.
Nauwt wunce did
he giv me chauwklit.
Boi yo boi,
nauwt evin did mouy
ahrange end poiple negleezhey
toiwn him awhn.
But still Oi put
coylas in mouy hayr
end Oi pouwr his couwfee
end ficks his dinna.
End Oi awlways seyz, 'Chawlie,
whadda ya duwin?'
End he awlways sez,
'Oim jus reedin tha paypa,
iz zat awl riyte wit choo?'

Survivor

After textiles, my father worked in futures.
He put away the squares of silk and cotton
and taught himself
to buy and sell a thing and never see it.
All abstraction, and then the dollar.
Every morning, he bit the lucky silver head.
He kept coins in dresser drawers,
suitcases of currency.

For him the world was a map
of circumstance and the Jew,
bullish and bearish,
only stalling tactics
until a new border guard.

And so when his wife died a natural death,
my father could not cry like one
who, entering the beloved temple,
sees the ark curtain torn away,
the Torah gone.
My father wept the bewildered tears
of one who had resolved
that even in a crashing market
there was a future
to be bought back at top dollar.

Poem

It's true, what they say,
love leaves you with scars.
I've still got the one on my back
from crawling beneath the barbed-
wire fence with you
to fuck in a cow pasture.

Poem

You with your constant hard-on, fucking
me everywhere, in backseats,
basements, farmers' fields, the ladies'
room, and once in your wife's bed.
I imagined every car I heard was her
coming home, but I never came that time.

Poem

"How do you like my cock?" he asks proudly,
grasping the member in question
firmly by the root.
I consider, remind myself
he's as innocent as G. A. Custer,
and me, an Indian.

Family Matters

Drunk, she held her first granddaughter.
The woman swayed and laughed, lifted the child up

at arm's length above her head. When she fell,
she fell in the slow motion in which all

accidents happen. Her son, who had just
entered the bedroom, caught his mother

around the waist; still, he, the baby,
and mother toppled together

onto the unmade safety of the bed.
In the end it was not the baby

he thought about—the baby would be fine—
but how he had to lift himself out from between

his mother's legs like a man.

A Married Man

The child showed what she
learned in school today.
Guess what this is, she said,
cracking both hands together
over her father's head
and running her fingers lightly
down the sides of his face.
"An egg?" he said.
No, your heart.

At Home

Finally they stopped speaking altogether.
He was silent. She was mute.
It was not for hostility or bitterness
But to avoid these they stopped,
For what he said hurt her
And what she spoke was anger.

They moved quite easily this way
Through days of small devotions
To each other. Nights she stifled
Her body's inevitable sounds, which,
Though pleasurable, would break
The illusion they lived in accord
And needed no speech,
That there was no ravine across which
They stretched and called,
No soil where gardens sprang up,
Not even the slight divide cats trace,
Anxious for food.

Summer came and went.
Soon only parts of the body were safe.
So they stayed, hand on neck,
Waiting to rise while larger actions
Shouted like cracked bells,
Lazarus and his wife born late.

Shirts

I toss them on the bed, a dozen dead man's shirts.
A gift from the widow, I can wear them to work.

I pull out the pins. Tissue sighs and falls.
Some shirts open like the wings of seagulls
sunning on rocks off the coast of Portugal in 1974.
Some open like the arms of a host striding toward
    you,
wondering who invited you.

I say this for Hurstwood's frayed collar.
I say this for his misplaced stud.
I say this for Gatsby's extravagance
of linen, of silk, of fine flannel.

I say this most of all for Mayakovsky,
for his knowledge of what is appropriate,
and against the siren song of the daily grind.

Fabian

The stories they told us are true.
They found him on a doorstep,
a kid, ordinary as the rest of us,
and made him a star though he couldn't
sing a lick, or just about could.
"Tiger" was okay. "Turn Me Loose" better.
Actually pretty good if contrived.

There will never be a Fabian cult.
He didn't die young. He outgrew his sweetness,
made a few movies, not much came of it.
We heard he beat his wife.
Now he's revived and tours with Bobby Rydell,
also of South Philly,
once praised by Sinatra.

He embodies for us aspects
of rock's democratic aspirations
as well as its capitalistic manipulations.
We all can do it and make a bundle,
or someone who does it may give
one of us who does not a token—
a long car or a lock of hair.

And he embodies as well a moment
we recall with increasing fondness
of restless boredom in postwar America
when Ike lay under sedation
and Jack Kennedy was on the make.

First Dog

First dog I remember was Ken Cameron's hound.
His old eyes—he was twice my age—suffered
my small hands hanging on his ears.

More love in that than in my house,
I'll tell you. We had no dog. There was some
reason—John Bray the neighbor's garden. Stupid
    lie—

you can tie a dog or make a fence or teach
a good dog where to go. There could have been
brown eyes that leveled love at mine.

And would a different child have grown
to mourn anyway for some other love never
    learned?
or have no poems seeking like lost dogs for love?

Foolish speculations! In this my only life,
spotted hound, I'm forever clutching at your fine
    ears,
forever searching your eyes for a loving look.

Amusing Prudence, Who's Recuperating from a Cut Foreleg

Here, Prudence, sniff this poem.
Sense my absence.
Where is the moon in this poem?
Where is the bone?
Why is everything so white
under the Dalmatian moon?

Where's Pete? Red meat!
thin-sliced at the deli—
"Sharp!" says steel to knife.
What red meat knows about
sharp edges—that's our main address.
We find each other home.

Heart on Campaign
(The Ballad of Lee Hart)

For every woman who's lived with shame,
borne responsibility, accepted blame,
or wondered where he went when he came:

this is for you, far from the covers
of *Time* and *People,* and from his lovers
(younger, sweeter); this is how you get over

what you never get over: the loss
of someone you love, and the cause.
For twenty-eight years I lived by one law:

the marriage of body and soul—
one mind, one mate—Gary was all
I wanted (did wanting make me small?).

Could I have pushed too far, too
hard and long? I thought I knew
him, would see him through

anything. But I'm tired of people
saying I'm strong, wishing me well.
Politics, my dear, *is lonely as hell.*

I lost him in the hopes of becoming
something greater. I'd give anything
to get my heart started running.

ELIZABETH LERNER

Collating

I was moving to the rhythm of the Xerox machine,
thrusting forward almost imperceptibly, deep in
the hips, with each page as it pushed through
the lubricated works, whooshing around the hot
     drum
and spitting itself out in the feeder
when I realized an Up and Coming editor
(mentioned in *Vanity Fair* and *Esquire*) was behind
me (his assistant away in a rehab),
waiting to use the copier. I blushed,
rushed to finish my job, and fled
the Xerox center. That night in bed I replayed
the scene: him doing me from behind, and a
     hundred
million copies of my memo (re: us fucking) came
flying out of the machine and landed, collated.

The Handicap

Love was a Yoo-Hoo mixed with cream soda
at the halfway house on the ninth hole
where my father let me drive the cart
(risking all club rules about a minor's
use) down a shaded lane where he leaned
over and kissed me clumsily on the lips.
It was all I needed: those few undaunted
moments to live my lifetime through
from every hot resinated drag off slow
burning joints in the suburban basements
with the parents home/not home, every fake
hit of acid (circa '76) that kept pockets
of teenagers speeding for hours on golf courses
that might have been heaven in the dewy glow
of dawn coming down, where I wondered
if anything could feel as lonely as
that abundance of parental love.

Mrs. Lensing

Mrs. Lensing, I'm not well;
this morning I could not find
my third hat since Christmas
and my dad had his coffee
without me. I looked
where I had lost that mitten
and a pocket knife last week,
where the hammer and shaving cream
and things and things
had gone. I found a book
inside a sweater I've outgrown,
with two letters from my mother
I left between pages 4 and 5.
This morning my coffee turned cold,
Mrs. Lensing; can I lie down?

PAUL K. SHEPHERD

New

I don't write fancy poetry,
in fact my stuff's not as good
as the old guys who never went
to school to write. I
do drink my coffee black,
and I've even been known to
do the hard stuff. But
this here, this one, is really
just saying how sorry I am
to be writing modern shit, the
very kind I hate, when we need
so much more old shit.

Ten Years Ago the Frozen Yogurt Guy

could not have (ten years ago
there was no frozen yogurt guy)
could not have told us last night,
"Our vanilla is down."

Geisha

Intrigued
the room
entered itself
with the tiny steps
of a mermaid
with a mustache
of orange blossom
with an abyss
dangling from
one pierced ear.

Women

Eating and going
to the bathroom
most of the time
it's cold
in the ladies' room
full of lines
& toilet paper
scattered from
seats of contagion
some joker
has locked empty inside.

Morning Toilette, Southwest China

In one of the villages that grow like colonies of brown mushrooms amid the terraced hillsides, a man in a stone house looks out at the sunrise that is reddening the tile roofs and their finials. He looks at the vegetable gardens, the fields of yellow rapeseed and purple vetch, the screens of narrow dark pine trees. He looks at the sky, already drained of color by the rising heat. Then he steps into the embroidered peach-silk river, which flows around his sepia limbs as he floats out to the well.

Beached Whale

This is not Nantucket of the whaling days, when whole villages turned out to wonder at such sights. But we New Yorkers are not unfamiliar with the crashing of bodies on our shores. This one is pearl-gray, stained with darker patches of sweat and dirt, eyes closed, shopping bags piled around his head, mouth spouting snores and saliva. His shirt buttons and the rope belt holding his trousers have opened away from his blue-white blubber, which is swelling and ebbing like a running sea, while incoming tides of office workers foam around him on the concrete beach.

Toy

It was a green windup tank with bright yellow treads running like twin belts along its sides. It moved with a thin little rattling noise. It also moved very fast, for a tank. Another interesting thing was that after traveling straight ahead for a while, it would veer off suddenly at an angle. Every few seconds its hatch cover would open, and a tin soldier would pop out, as far as his waist, and look around. He was wearing a khaki uniform and helmet, and a long, fringed, white silk scarf that waved behind him in the make-believe wind. Holding binoculars to his eyes, he scanned the room, his head moving from side to side with small jerking movements. Then he slid back into the tank, and the hatch cover closed over him. This went on until the day the cover closed down too soon, cutting off the soldier's head, which fell to the floor. The blood gushed up out of his body with such force that it blasted the hatch cover right off the tank.

I Can't Write This

I can't write this
I'm too busy
looking
for a girl
to give me the look
just so I know
I have her
so I can go on
with this
which I can't
if I don't even know
when
and where
I'm going to get
it
this look
this girl
so I can't be
looking for words
to say
I can't do this
sitting with my dick
with many
sets of tits
at my table
leaving me
no room
to write this.

Medical Ethics

The man was lying there in restraints,
his beard like messed pubic hair.
The rubbing alcohol he drank made

his breath hot and his body cool. The doctor
turned him with a long arm and distant nose.
He had seen more harm

come to people in one night; he supposed
enough. He thought of his wife,
and the antics they could have

at home, and he rolled the man back.
Then he hit the man, fast,
low, with the curtain closed,

and his fist closed,
and ascribed it to the course of things.

Red Wash

She came out with naked heels
and perfect teeth, and was fragile

in between. Our studies, each
in its own way unbearable, reached

for her darkness in rubbed charcoals.
There were no comments, no

other figures, no need to place her,
and after hours we drank together.

One day, hesitant and sad, she
came out in panties,

then retired. We had hired naked
women only, who never bled.

Married Life as a Controlled Substance

We kissed a little, did more a lot.
I lied to get possession of her,
said I had no bad habits.
On the way we slipped and glided.
Here's the danger:

she allows me everything
so long as I reach the high-
up stuff and keep in training
for the good life. I bathe
heavily and let my eyes

shape themselves to new
facts. I comment when I'm charmed.
Like when she threw
her hips around last night
and I got sleepy and real harm-

less. I'll never move
out, I told her. Trust that.
What does all this prove?
That you remember details
when a doctor asks.

I never look like myself

Dear Professor X:

Thank you for your letter inviting me to Germany to participate in a conference on current "German-Jewish relations" in the aftermath of the Holocaust, initiated and organized by distinguished Jewish Americans, yourself among them, and joined on your letterhead by other Americans of distinction and by prominent Germans of good will. It is very kind of you to have had me in mind; I am touched by your generosity and trust. I wish my response could be simpler than it is destined to be. In a sense, it is simple enough: I am already committed to an event that will take place in New York during the period of the conference. But to tell you that, and to leave it at that, would hardly be candid.

Professor X, I am a Jew who does not, will not, cannot, set foot in Germany. This is a private moral imperative; I don't think of it as a "rule," and I don't apply it to everyone, particularly not to German-born Jews, who as refugees or survivors have urgencies and exigencies different from my own. Not to set foot in Germany is for me, and I think for many garden-variety Jewish Americans like myself, one of the few possible memorials; and it seems to me unsurprising that in this connection a memorial should take the form of a negation, a turning away.

But there is another point of view as well, one that may be more relevant here. Yours is the fourth invitation I have had to go to Germany. Each was issued with the best will in the world: a German hand reaching out in peace from a democratic German polity—a remembering hand, never a forgetful one. The hand of the "new generation." The more that hand reaches out in its remembering remorsefulness, in its hopeful good will, the more resistant my heart becomes.

Here is why. I believe that all this—the conscientious memorializing of what happened four and five decades ago to the Jewish citizens of Germany and of Europe—is in the nature of things an insular and parochial German task. It is something for the Germans to do, independently, in the absence of Jews—the absence of Jews in contemporary Germany being precisely the point. The German task is, after all, a kind of "liberation" (of conscience into history), or emancipation, and the only genuine emancipation—as we know from many other national, social, and cultural contexts—is autoemancipation. So when Germans want to reflect on German-Jewish "reconciliation," or—skirting that loaded word—"German-Jewish relations," it seems to me they are obligated to do it on their own. Does that strike you as impossible, if not absurd? A bit of nonsense out of Lewis Carroll? A hand held out in friendship to someone who isn't there? How can "relations" with Jews be achieved in the absence of Jews? Well, that's exactly the difficulty, isn't it? Europe no longer has what it used to call its "Jewish problem," the Germans having solved it with finality. But there remains now a German problem—the ongoing, perhaps infinitely protracted, problem of the German national conscience—and its gravamen is that the Jews aren't there.

It appears that what Germans of good will have been doing lately—and more and more they are doing it with the aid and counsel of American Jewish organizations—is evading the tumultuous epicenter of the problem, even as they struggle to offer more and more evidence that they are facing it. There are no native-born Jews over fifty to achieve "relations" with. Germany is a Jewish museum: apartments, furniture, old neighborhoods newly populated; the old headstones that survived vandalism in the museum-cemeteries or were heaped up as rubble barriers against tanks. Not the old synagogues, though; these were mainly burned. If an old volume by a popular author of the twenties turns up, it has the antiquarian interest of a rare book: books by Jewish writers were burned in every public square—who doesn't know this? The notion of a Jew as a kind of surprising vestige or anachronism—as, in fact, an actual museum piece—is apparently pervasive in Germany, and was once brought home to me by a representative of a German publisher who, after a conversation in New York, wrote me a warmly intended letter: *My time with you was different from any other experience; it was like a visit to a museum.* The handful of Jews—scarce items!—who today live in pitiful numbers in Berlin or Frankfurt are, however they may view themselves, futureless, deluded, lost to history or sense or any purpose except, perhaps, the immediacy of opportunism. Prime Minister Kohl likes to remind the world that he was only twelve at the end of the war—meaning, he wants us to understand, that he wasn't implicated in the making of Nazism; but of course Nazism was implicated in the making of Kohl, unless you suppose that early schooling, from kindergarten to the seventh grade, has no effect at all on a human mind. By the time Kohl was twelve, he had long ago seen the last of any Jewish child in his classroom. Nine-tenths of the German Jewish twelve-year-olds of Kohl's generation (and of mine) were transmuted into bonemeal; a few who escaped turned up in school with me in New York.

Mournfully, it needs to be said again: there are no native-born Jews of my generation for contemporary Germans to seek "relations" with. A perplexity; an obstacle, one might conclude. The German solution has been to behave according to a commonplace analogy, pragmatically inspired, perhaps, by the straightforward realm of international economics; of demand and scarcity. If your country has no bauxite, say—if your country through its own folly has depleted its native supply of bauxite—what do you do? Naturally you import some bauxite from another country where bauxite is in plentiful supply, and you pay out whatever is necessary to bring in what suits your purpose. And if you have depleted through your own folly your native (and plentiful) supply of Jews, and now you feel remorseful, what do you do? You put an order in to America—which, rather than depleting its supply of Jewish citizens, has nourished and multiplied it—and you import living foreign Jews to stand in for the native missing Jews.

I am afraid that all such programs—wherein Jewish Americans offer themselves (always out of the ideals of humaneness, reconciliation, hope for the future) to stand in for the murdered Jews of Europe—are mistaken at the core, and in any case cannot help the Germans. The Germans must undertake memorial explorations under their given condition of scarcity—the absence of native Jews. Why must an American writer, a Jewish citizen of the United States, be imported for a conference on "German-Jewish relations"? Only because there is no German-born Jewish writer of her own age who is alive to speak. So a foreign surrogate must do.

But it seems to me that this principle of surrogacy is conceived in profound error. Who will dare to suggest that any living Jew can offer reconciliation—or even simple human presence—on behalf of the murdered?

Then let Germans of good will do it on their own. For starters, they, not American Jewish sponsors, should be the organizing spirits behind Holocaust conferences on German soil—conferences by and for Germans. Is the so-called *Kristallnacht* (a Nazi term, by the way, signifying the shattering of the "crystal" mythically owned in vast abundance by the Jewish rich) a day of national mourning and memorial in present-day democratic Germany? Has anyone ever suggested such an idea? *Kristallnacht* happened to Jews—Jews were its victims; but *Kristallnacht* is by no means a Jewish issue. It is an issue of German culture, and certainly appropriate for examination by German institutions and conferences; but not, in my view, with the assistance or participation of foreign Jews. I visualize a German Haggadah of Lamentation written for an annual German seder of sorts, at which a dish of bonemeal is held up and the leader of the seder chants: "This is the ash of affliction which our fathers and mothers extracted from the torment, slavery, and slaughter of their sisters and brothers, even unto the littlest child . . ."

In brief, here is an instance where "reconciliation" and "relations" may not, cannot, be a collaborative act, i.e., a project between Germans and Jews, belonging equally (or even unequally) to both. Because if it appears to be collaborative, the act becomes a lie. The Germans in truth have no one to "collaborate" with but phantoms—the missing, the murdered, the Jews *not there,* the classmates of the twelve-year-old Kohl. Living Jewish Americans can't serve as surrogates. Anne Frank, before the Annex, before the flight to Holland, was a German Jew: had Germany not given its allegiance to the criminals and programs that murdered her, who can doubt that she would today have been a luminary of German letters? Which American writer can stand in for Anne Frank? Human beings are not bauxite; one bundle of Jews is not interchangeable with another bundle. The Nazis objectified Jews and made them interchangeable bundles. Ah, the bitterness of the irony that, in the name of "German-Jewish relations," in the name of good will and the hope of present and future humaneness, the interchangeability of one group of Jews with another is still being pursued on German soil!

An American writer who rode the subway in everyday freedom on her way to a New York high school between 1942 and 1945 can't take the place of a murdered German-Jewish writer born in the same year—an adolescent gassed in the very hour the unscathed American, studying high-school German, was learning to recite *"Röslein auf der Heiden."* That, I think, is the German dilemma; and that is what the "concerned Germans and Americans" on your letterhead need to come to grips with. When Jewish Americans go to Germany to "help"—i.e., to supply Jewish representation at a Holocaust conference—they aren't making it easier for the Germans to see into the soul of the dilemma, namely the loss of *German-Jewish* repre-

sentation; the Americans are confusing the question by abet-
ting the tragic and degrading falsehood of human interchangeability.

I am sorry to be so astringent. I have thought about these
matters for a long time, and with growing distress as the
decades pass and more and more American Jewish organizations fly to Germany in search of similar collaborative objec-
tives. Your letter, by the way, arrives on the very day another
letter has come to me, this one from a German university—a
warm and impressive and earnest letter from an extremely
able Ph.D. student (I judge this from the intelligent voice of
her fine English sentences) who is interested in fiction written
by Jewish Americans, and who has settled on my work as the
subject of her dissertation. A self-described "special case"
because of her preoccupation with American Jewish writing,
she sketches her family background: "My father became a
soldier when he was seventeen. His father was a theologian of
the Protestant Church and had the position of superintendent.
Even though my father's father began to mistrust the National
Socialists quite early in the thirties, he was a patriot and thus
sent four sons into the war. Three of them were killed." Three
dead uncles. I grieve at the obtuseness of this. With all the
good will in the world, my young correspondent (born in
1955) remains incapable of understanding that a German "patriot" would, at least in his heart if not in his (by then, let us
try to concede, coerced) actions, acknowledge that to fight for
Hitler was not German patriotism but a betrayal of Germany.
And this from a "theologian of the Protestant Church," in an
atmosphere of rampant official anti-Semitism. To whom, I
can't help wondering, did this theologian give his vote? Was
his "mistrust" of the Nazis "early in the thirties" a feeling of
immediate alarm and peril, or one of ballot-box regret after
the damage was done? My correspondent is clearly engaged,
from her point of view, in an intellectual project of remorse
and restitution; and yet she cannot recognize the most funda-
mental first necessity—an understanding of what patriotism

CYNTHIA OZICK

means: that it is something you do for yourself, by yourself, out
of obligation to the moral improvement of your country; that
it is above all a dream of self-transformation. It would be
better all around if she would neglect the study of "American
Jewish fiction" and begin a cultural meditation on her grandfather's mind. Q

Every year I bury one hundred and fifty of my townspeople. Another dozen or two I take to the crematory to be burned. I sell caskets, burial vaults, and urns for the ashes. I have a sideline in headstones and monuments. I do flowers on commission.

Apart from the tangibles, I sell the use of my building: eleven thousand square feet, furnished and fixtured with an abundance of pastel and chair rail and crown moldings. The whole lash-up is mortgaged and remortgaged well into the next century. My rolling stock includes a hearse, a limo, two Fleetwoods, and a mini-van with darkened windows our price list calls a service vehicle and everyone in town calls the Dead Wagon.

I used to use the "unit pricing method"—the old package deal. It meant you had only one number to look at. It was a large number. Now everything is itemized. It's the law. So now there is a long list of items and numbers and italicized disclaimers, something like a menu or the Sears, Roebuck wish book, and sometimes the federally mandated options begin to look like cruise control or rear-window defrost. I wear black most of the time, to keep folks in mind of the fact we're not talking Buicks here. At the bottom of the list there is still a large number.

In a good year the gross is close to half a million, 5 percent of which we hope to call profit. I am the only undertaker in this town. I have a corner on the market.

The market, such as it is, is figured on what is called the "crude death rate"—the number of deaths every year out of every thousand of persons.

Here is how it works.

Imagine a large room into which you coax one thousand people. You slam the doors in January, leaving them plenty of food and drink, color TVs, magazines, condoms. Your sample should have an age distribution heavy on Baby Boomers and their children—1.2 children per boomer. For every four normal people, there is one Old-Timer, who, if he or she wasn't in this big room, would probably be in Florida or Arizona or a nursing home. You get the idea. The group will include fifteen lawyers, one faith healer, three dozen real-estate agents, a video technician, several licensed counselors, and an Amway distributor. The rest will be between jobs, middle managers, ne'er-do-wells, or retired.

Now the magic part—come late December, when you throw open the doors, only 991.3, give or take, will shuffle out upright. Two hundred and sixty will now be selling Amway. The other 8.7 have become the crude death rate.

Here's another stat.

Of the 8.7 corpses, two-thirds will have been Old-Timers, 5 percent will be children, and the rest (2.75) will be Boomers—realtors and attorneys—one of whom was, no doubt, elected to public office during the year. What's more, three will have died of cerebral vascular or coronary difficulties, two of cancer, one each of vehicular mayhem, diabetes, and domestic violence. The spare change will be by act of God or suicide—most likely the faith healer.

The figure most often and most conspicuously missing from the insurance charts and demographics is the one I call THE BIG ONE, which refers to the number of people out of every one hundred born who will die. Over the long haul, THE BIG ONE hovers right around . . . well—dead nuts on 100. If this were on the charts, they would call it "Death expectancy" and no one would buy futures of any kind. But it is a useful number and has its lessons. Maybe you will want to figure out what to do with your life. Maybe it will make you feel a certain kinship to the rest of us. Maybe it will make you hysterical. Whatever the implications of a one hundred death expectancy, calculate how big a town this is and why mine produces for me steady, if sometimes unpredictable, labor.

They die around the clock here, without apparent preference for a day of the week, month of the year; there is no clear favorite in the way of season. Nor does the alignment of the stars, fullness of moon, or liturgical calendar have very much to do with it. The whereabouts are neither here nor there. They go off upright or horizontally, in Chevrolets and nursing homes, in bathtubs, on the interstates, in ERs, ORs, BMWs. And while it may be so that we assign more equipment or more importance to deaths that create themselves in places marked by initials—ICU being somehow better than Greenbrier Convalescent Home—it is also true that the dead don't care. In this way, the dead I bury and burn are like the dead before them, for whom time and space have become mortally unimportant. This loss of interest is, in fact, one of the first sure signs that something serious is about to happen. The next thing is they quit breathing. At this point, to be sure, a "gunshot wound to the chest" or "shock and trauma" will get more ink than a CVA or ASHD, but no condition of death is any less permanent than any other. All will do. The dead don't care.

Nor does *who* much matter, either. To say "I'm okay, you're okay, and by the way, he's dead!" is, for the living, a kind of comfort.

It is why we drag rivers and comb plane wrecks.

It is why MIA is more painful than DOA.

It is why we have open caskets and classified obits.

Knowing is better than not knowing, and knowing it is you is terrifically better than knowing it is me. Once I'm the dead guy, whether you're okay or he's okay won't much interest me. You can both go bag your asses, because the dead don't care.

Of course, the living, bound by their adverbs and their actuarials, still do. Now there's the difference and why I'm in business. The living are careful and oftentimes caring. The dead are careless, or maybe it's care-less. Either way, they don't care. These are unremarkable and verifiable truths.

My former mother-in-law, herself an unremarkable and verifiable truth, was always fond of holding forth with Cagneyesque bravado—to wit, "When I'm dead, just put me in a box and throw me in a hole." But whenever I would remind her that we did substantially that with *everyone*, the woman would grow sullen and a little cranky.

Later, over meat loaf and green beans, she would invariably give out with "When I'm dead, just cremate me and scatter the ashes."

My former mother-in-law was trying to make carelessness sound like fearlessness. The kids would stop eating and look at each other. The kids' mother would whine, "Oh, Mom, don't talk like that." I'd take out my lighter and begin to play with it.

In the same way, the priest that married me to this woman's daughter—a man who loved golf and gold ciboria and vestments made of Irish linen; a man who drove a great black sedan with a wine-red interior and who always had his eye on the cardinal's job—this same fellow, leaving the cemetery one day, felt called upon to instruct me thus: "No bronze coffin for me. No sir! No orchids or roses or limousines. The plain pine box is the one I want, a quiet Low Mass, and the pauper's grave. No pomp or circumstance."

He wanted, he explained, to be an example of simplicity, of prudence, of piety and austerity—all priestly and, apparently, Christian virtues. When I told him that he needn't wait, that he could begin his ministry of good example yet today, that he could quit the country club and do his hacking at the public links and trade his brougham for a used Chevette, that free of his Florsheims and cashmeres and prime ribs, free of his bingo nights and building funds, he could become, for Christ's sake, the very incarnation of Francis himself, or Anthony of Padua; when I said, in fact, that I would be willing to assist him in this, that I would gladly distribute his CDs and credit cards among the needy of the parish, and that I would, when the sad duty called, bury him for nothing in the manner he would have by then become accustomed to; when I told the priest who had married me these things, he said nothing at all, but turned his wild eye on me in the manner in which the cleric must have looked on Sweeney years ago, before he cursed him, irreversibly, into a bird.

What I was trying to tell the fellow was, of course, that being a dead saint is no more worthwhile than being a dead philodendron or a dead angelfish. Living is the rub, and always has been. Living saints still feel the flames and stigmata, the ache of chastity and the pangs of conscience. Once dead, they let their relics do the legwork, because, as I was trying to tell this priest, the dead don't care.

Only the living care.

And I am sorry to be repeating myself, but this is the central fact of my business—that there is nothing, once you are dead, that can be done *to you* or *for you* or *with you* or *about you* that will do you any good or any harm; that any damage or decency we do accrues to the living, to whom your death happens if it really happens to anyone. The living have to live with it; you don't. Theirs is the grief or gladness your death brings. And there is the truth, abundantly self-evident, that seems, now that I think of it, the one most elusive to my old in-laws, to the parish priest, and to perfect strangers who are forever accosting me in barbershops and in cocktail bars and at parent-teacher conferences, hell-bent or duty-bound on telling me what it is they want done with them when they are dead.

Give it a rest is the thing I say.

Once you are dead, put your feet up, call it a day, and let the old man or the missus or the thankless kids decide whether you are to be buried or burned or blown out of a cannon or left to dry out in a ditch. It's not your day to watch it, because the dead don't care.

Another reason people are always rehearsing their obse-

quies with me has to do with the fear of death, which is something anyone in his right mind has. It is healthy. It keeps us
from playing in the traffic. I say pass it on to the kids.

There is a belief—widespread among the women I have
dated, local Rotarians, and friends of my children—that I,
being the undertaker here, have some irregular fascination
with, special interest in, inside information about, even attach-
ment to, *the dead.* They assume, these people, some perhaps
with good reason, that I want their bodies.

It is an interesting concept.

But here's the truth.

Being dead is one—the worst, the last—but only one in a
series of calamities that afflicts our own and several other
species. The list may include, but is not limited to, gingivitis,
bowel obstruction, contested divorce, tax audit, spiritual vexa-
tion, money trouble, political mischief, and on and on and on.
There is no shortage of *misery.* And I am no more attracted to
the dead than the dentist is to your bad gums, the doctor to
your rotten innards, or the accountant to your sloppy expense
records. I have no more stomach for misery than the banker
or the lawyer, the pastor or the politico—because misery is
careless and is everywhere. Misery is the bad check, the ex-
wife, the mob in the street, and the IRS—who, like the dead,
feel nothing and, like the dead, *don't care.*

Which is not to say that the dead do not matter.

They do.

Last Monday morning, Milo Hornsby died. Mrs. Hornsby
called at 2:00 A.M. to say that Milo had "expired" and would
I take care of it, as if his condition were like any other that
could be renewed or somehow improved upon. At 2:00 A.M.,
yanked from sleep, I am thinking, Put a quarter in Milo and call
me in the morning. But Milo is dead. In a moment, in a twinkling, Milo has slipped irretrievably out of our reach, beyond
Mrs. Hornsby and the children, beyond the women at the
laundromat he owned, beyond his comrades at the Legion
Hall, the Grand Master of the Masonic Lodge, his pastor at

First Baptist, beyond the mailman, zoning board, town council, and Chamber of Commerce; beyond us all, and any treachery or any kindness we had in mind for him.

Milo is dead.

X's on his eyes, lights out, curtains.

Helpless, harmless.

Milo's dead.

Which is why I do not haul to my senses, coffee and a quick shave, Homburg and great coat, warm up the Dead Wagon, and make for the freeway in the early o'clock for Milo's sake but for his missus's sake, for she who has become, in the same moment and same twinkling, like water to ice, the widow Hornsby. I go for her—because she still can cry and care and pray and pay my bill.

The hospital that Milo died in is state of the art. There are signs on every door declaring a part or process or bodily function. I like to think that, taken together, the words would add up to something like the Human Condition, but they never do. What's left of Milo, the remains, are in the basement, between SHIPPING & RECEIVING and LAUNDRY ROOM. Milo would like that if he were still liking anything. Milo's room is called PATHOLOGY.

The medical-technical parlance of death emphasizes disorder. We are forever dying of failures, of anomalies, of insufficiencies, of dysfunctions, arrests, accidents. These are either chronic or acute. The language of death certificates—Milo's says "Cardiopulmonary Failure"—is like the language of weakness. Likewise, Mrs. Hornsby, in her grief, will be said to be breaking down or falling apart or going to pieces, as if there were something structurally awry with her. It is as if death and grief were not part of the Order of Things, as if Milo's failure and his widow's weeping were, or ought to be, sources of embarrassment. "Doing well" for Mrs. Hornsby would mean that she is bearing up, braving the storm, or being strong for the children. We have willing pharmacists to help her with this. Of course, for Milo, doing well would mean he was back upstairs, holding his own, keeping the meters and monitors bleeping.

But Milo is downstairs, between SHIPPING & RECEIVING and LAUNDRY ROOM, in a stainless-steel drawer, wrapped in white plastic top to toe, and—because of his small head, wide shoulders, ponderous belly, and skinny legs, and the trailing white binding cord from his ankles and toe tags—he looks, for all the world, like a larger than life-size sperm.

I sign for him and get him out of there. At some level, I am still thinking Milo gives a shit, which by now we all know he doesn't—because the dead don't care.

Back at my place of business, upstairs in the embalming room, behind a door marked PRIVATE, Milo Hornsby is floating on a porcelain table under fluorescent lights. Unwrapped, outstretched, Milo is beginning to look a little more like himself—eyes wide open, mouth agape, returning to our gravity. I shave him, close his eyes, his mouth. We call this "setting the features." These are the features—eyes and mouth—that, in death, will never look the way they would look in life, when they are always opening, closing, focusing, signaling, telling us something. In death, what they tell us is they will not be doing anything anymore. The last detail to be managed is Milo's hands—one folded over the other, over the umbilicus, in an attitude of ease, of repose, of retirement.

They will not be doing anything anymore, either.

I wash his hands before positioning them.

When my wife moved out some years ago, I kept the children and the dirty laundry. It was big news in a small town. There was the gossip and the goodwill that places like this are famous for. And while there was plenty of talk, no one knew exactly what to say to me. They felt helpless, I suppose. So they brought casseroles and beef stews, took the kids out to the movies or canoeing, brought their younger sisters around to visit me. What Milo did was send his laundry van by twice a week for two months, until I had found a housekeeper. Milo would pick up five loads in the morning and return them by lunchtime, fresh and folded. I never asked him to do this. I hardly knew him. I had never been in his home or in his laundromat. His wife had never known my wife. His children were too old to play with my children.

After my housekeeper was installed, I went to thank Milo and to pay my bill. The invoices detailed the number of loads, the washers and the dryers, detergent, bleaches, fabric softeners. I think the total came to sixty dollars. When I asked Milo what the charges were for pickup and delivery, for stacking and folding, for saving my life and the lives of my children, for keeping us in clean clothes and towels and bed linens, "Never mind that," Milo said, "one hand washes the other."

I place Milo's right hand over his left hand, then try the other way. Then back again. Then I decide that it does not matter, that one hand washes the other either way.

The embalming takes me about two hours.

It is daylight by the time I am done.

Every Monday morning Paddy Fulton comes to my office. He was damaged in some profound way in Korea. The details of his damage are unknown to the locals. Paddy Fulton has no limp or anything missing—so everyone thinks it was something he saw in Korea that left him a little simple, occasionally perplexed, the type to draw rein abruptly in his day-long walks, to consider the meaning of litter, pausing over bottle caps and gum wrappers. Paddy Fulton has a nervous smile and a dead-fish handshake. He wears a baseball cap and thick eyeglasses. Every Sunday night Paddy goes to the I.G.A. and buys up the tabloids at the checkout stands with headlines that usually involve Siamese twins or movie stars or UFOs. Paddy is a speed reader and a math whiz—but because of his damage, he has never held a job and never applied for one.

Every Monday morning, Paddy brings me clippings of stories under headlines like: 601 LB. MAN FALLS THRU COFFIN—A GRAVE SITUATION or EMBALMER FOR THE STARS SAYS ELVIS IS FOREVER. The Monday morning Milo died, Paddy's clipping had to do with an urn full of ashes that made grunting and groaning noises, that whistled sometimes, and that was expected to begin talking. Certain scientists in England could make no sense of it. They had run several tests. The ashes' widow, however—left with nine children and no estate—is convinced that her dearly beloved and greatly reduced husband is trying to give her winning numbers for the lottery. "Jacky would never leave us without good prospects," she says. "He loved his family more than anything." There is a picture of the two of them—the widow and the urn, the living and the dead, flesh and bronze, the Victrola and the Victrola's dog. She has her ear cocked, waiting.

We are always waiting. Waiting for some good word or for the winning numbers. Waiting for a sign or wonder, some signal from our dear dead that the dead still care. We are gladdened when they do outstanding things, when they arise from their graves or appear to us in dreams or fall from their caskets. It pleases us no end, as if there were no end; as if the dead still cared, had agendas, were yet alive.

But the sad and well-known fact of the matter is that most of us will stay in our caskets and be dead a long time, and that our urns and graves will never make a sound. Our reason and requiems, our headstones and High Masses, will neither get us in nor keep us out of heaven. The meaning of our lives, and the memories of them, will belong only to the living, just as our funerals do.

We heat graves here for winter burials, as a kind of foreplay before digging in, to loosen the frost's hold on the ground before the sexton and his backhoe do the opening. We buried Milo in the ground last Wednesday. It was, by then, the only thing to do. The mercy is that what we buried there, in an oak casket, just under the frost line, had ceased to be Milo. It was something else. Milo had become the idea of himself, a permanent fixture of the third person and past tense, his widow's loss of appetite and trouble sleeping, the absence in places where we look for him, our habits of him breaking, our phantom limb, our one hand washing the other. **Q**

[1]

Upstairs at McDonald's, on West Third Street. Bright morning light pours in through the floor-to-ceiling windows. Outside, a slight wind ripples the flag above the Blue Note, JAZZ capital of the world. Inside, the speakers fill the space with upbeat electronic slang, buoying the spirits of the solitary coffee sippers, staring at the plastic lids of their Styrofoam cups. Pairs of teenagers come and go, talking of Fra Angelico, no.

It's time to write something funny. Lately, my stories have all been explicitly about death, or implicitly about conquering death through out-of-character acts. Morbidity is all right, but enough is enough. Real, living plants, well tended, hang from chains and hooks, partially obscuring, from my vantage point, the exit sign's red block letters. Fragments of conversation drift diffidently, mostly obscured by the squeak of Egg McMuffin cartons and the strains of "Mack the Knife."

It's time to write something funny. Where, in the depths of my experience, does comedy reside? Where are the depths of my experience? Below, bicycles roll by, a man in a blue shirt, a woman in green shorts, a retarded boy in a Yankee cap with a spastic gait, not keeping pace with a beautiful mixed-race child in a stroller.

Fame and fortune. American dreams with which I've always been infected, like a good American, as I've drifted, unimaginatively, from career to career, from city to city, always feeling like a fish out of water; as I've mourned my father, crippled by a stroke since his eighteenth year, and my restless mother, and my brother, passively waiting for life's signposts to tick by. Fame and fortune. There's a fit subject for comedy, I think.

There's an unshakable conviction among certain Americans, or all Americans, that they possess a certain spark, a certain glimmer of genius, of greatness, a certain something that would emerge, if only for a moment, for all the world to see, if circumstances were right, if conditions and luck permitted, which they almost never do. I have friends, New York is full of such people, with their convictions; and now also Hoboken and Jersey City. Waitresses who are really dancers, waiting to dance; probation officers who are really artists, painting on the side; computer salespeople who write songs waiting to be sold and sung. And pitying all those other people who are just what they are, waitresses or probation officers, accountants with wives and children, just doing their jobs well and bringing home their paychecks and loving their families. What empty lives.

Me, I'm a lawyer, sort of. For now. Until the loans are paid off, until my ship comes in, until I win the lottery, until I'm discovered. I'm admitted to practice law in six states and the District of Columbia, and I've practiced in all of them. Each new job has given me slightly longer vacations, slightly shorter hours. Slightly more time to do what I really do. I'm a lawyer, but actually I'm a writer of stories and, someday perhaps, of novels.

But do not misunderstand me. In common with certain Americans, or all Americans, I realize that all I possess is a glimmer, a spark, that I'm neither Hawthorne nor Henry James, those full-timers of talent. One or two stories a year, that's my quota, corresponding to my one or two ideas a year. Some years a little more, some a little less. Not always brilliant ideas, either, as I realize in retrospect or halfway through, or now.

But better than no ideas at all, certainly. The funny thing is, quite unexpectedly, just about when I had given up hope, and altogether run out of ideas, there I was:

Discovered.

[11]

The pace picks up around lunchtime. Hordes of Hispanics, quick Quarter Pounders, rapid table turnover as the air conditioner moves into high gear. In the morning, you clear your own table, drop your debris in the container marked *Thank You.* At noon, attendants, attentive to your last swallow, come for your tray, let you know it's time to move on. You have to stare through them, at the handball court where the eyes of bare-chested black men strain to pick up the little black ball coming out of the graffiti. Still, there's no better place to write.

I've been writing, in fast-food establishments, among strangers, for years and years, slowly and unmethodically, those little squeeze packets of ketchup, I would imagine, my major source of inspiration. During these same years, I have watched the Supreme Court, whose work I follow with fading interest, expand and then contract the Fourth Amendment, and then the Fifth. The Court too, estranged from its past, I have to assume, does most of its opinion writing in Wendy's.

What at first appears to be a naturally occurring spattering of yellow on the well-tended leaves proves to be dried mustard, no longer fragrant. I've been writing these things for years and years, and sending them off. First, to *The New Yorker,* the quickest ticket to success. Sometimes, so it has seemed, the editors, with a sixth sense, have anticipated my submissions: on occasion, I've gotten rejection slips for stories not yet written. Cream-colored, five by seven slips of paper, reminding, in parentheses, that all submissions should be accompanied by return postage.

Once, along with my story, I received back someone else's, also rejected—a piece about a motorcycle accident and a brain transplant. The clobbered mind of the deceased replaced with his grandfather's, somewhat more intact. Soon the boy's body has begun to wither and his thoughts have turned to Calvin Coolidge. The process cannot be reversed. If only the writer had done some preliminary research using rats, she would have known, and the whole debacle could have been avoided.

After *The New Yorker,* I send them to a random sample of those literary magazines. This *Review,* that *Review,* the ones named after streets and regions long since deserted, and colleges and obscure mythological things. It's easy enough to lose heart collecting those preprinted five-by-sevens, but then there are always grounds for encouragement. Out in the wilderness, you look for signs. An unusually delayed rejection must mean a near-miss; a handwritten "Sorry" at least means somebody read it and liked it. And there are friends willing to pronounce each new one the best yet, in exchange for reciprocal recognition. But with your friends you never know.

This past year, working, uncharacteristically, in fried-chicken places, I wrote two very short pieces. In print, taken together, no more than four pages. Surely some magazine could spare four pages. I sent them out as a package. In addition to the usual random sample, I selected a little publication I'd never noticed before. What the hell, what's to lose?

[I I I]

You listen long enough, you'd be amazed at what comes out of those concealed speakers. Famous fragments of Beethoven's Fifth spliced into Tchaikovsky's Sixth followed by Coleman Hawkins. Something by Tom Waits, off the *Blue Valentine* album. All part of the cultural infrastructure. Today, the stairs up are blocked by a broom handle and I'm stuck at street level.

Down here, the desperate characters linger interminably over a coffee and a borrowed cigarette, and carefully wipe out the cup before depositing it in the shopping bag on the adjacent seat. They must know that upstairs is reserved for the real customers, like me. An old woman asks the manager for a listing of every McDonald's in Manhattan. Funny they don't have a preprinted list. He has to write it out, from the phone book. So few on the Upper East Side, the woman laments.

Consider the potentialities residing in a plastic packet of ketchup. Tiny red pool. Flexible, supple skin enclosing moist entrails. Palpated, amoeba-like, it changes shape; ruptured, human-like, it bleeds.

Some kind of strange hick sits down at the table next to mine. Blue duffel bag, badly faded, dirty jeans, a green skull tattooed on his forearm, shoulder-length oily blond hair beneath a shallow leather cap, unhealthy skin, brown teeth widely spaced. "Winston Lights! You're not gonna believe this, I used to smoke Winston 100s." I offer him my pack. I only smoke when I write.

From the blue sack he fishes a somewhat rumpled sheet of loose-leaf paper. "Look closely. How many faces can you find? Look carefully. Take as long as you want." The page contains a geometric design, all triangles and squares, in red, green, blue, yellow, and brown pencil. Farther down, in light gray pencil, barely legible, barely visible, ornamentation of an earlier vintage, a cold-cut order: half pound ham, quarter pound American.

I indicate the fruits of my search. Four pairs of small blue triangular heads with square red eyes, which, seen from a broader perspective, form the chins of four pairs of larger, multicolored faces. "No, look some more. There are Chinamen with beards, see? And pirates. Cutthroats and spacemen, here and here. See the eagle? Here's the beak. This picture took me exactly two hours and fourteen minutes, from start to finish. I never use a ruler. I always start from a *single dot* in the center, and work from there."

I hand back the drawing.

"I've been an artist for exactly three months, two days, and five hours. I'm still an amateur, but my horoscope predicted I'd be making some money soon; 'a financial opportunity on the horizon,' it said. Maybe today's my lucky day." Extracting a blank sheet from his bag, and consulting his watch, he begins a new picture, a single black dot, quickly surrounded by eight more, forming a square. Across from him, next to me, sits his fat, bearded, silent partner, reading the *Daily News.* Perhaps to these two, ketchup is a vegetable.

Sometimes, even down here, among strangers, you see something to give you courage. A pale, thick-bespectacled Eastern European with his much darker grandson, the two playing with toy cars. A spilled cup of Coke. No tragedy, its flow contained by the expansion joints between the amber floor tiles.

My two little pieces steadily garnered for me the customary quota of thank-you-but-no-thank-yous. Last to respond was the new little publication I'd never noticed before. A thick envelope could mean only one thing. But no, not exactly. Together with my stories was a handwritten note: "Let's see what else you have. And send these two along as well." Two dollars in postage stamps. My first remuneration for my writing.

What could this mean? I hadn't been rejected, but I hadn't been accepted, either. I was still in the competition. I chose three more stories and sent them off, along with the original two.

Now seems as good a time as any to register my disapproval of the nomination of Robert Bork to the Supreme Court. By the way, in a couple of hours I'm supposed to get married.

[I V]

Roy Rogers, on Court Street in Brooklyn, between Remsen and Montague, down the block from my new job. The air-conditioning works a little too well, the hanging lamps cast too sharp a shadow, the recorded music tends too much toward the tinny, but there are fewer distractions than in the McDonald's, two blocks down, on Livingston.

Funny I should wind up in the D.A.'s office. I never pictured myself a prosecutor, always having been infected with a Warren Court liberalism, an orientation in favor of criminal defendants. But the fringe benefits are hard to beat. Thirty-six paid holidays, from the founding of the New York Public Library to Zoroaster's birthday. And besides, I'm not really a prosecutor. Actually, I'm a writer. Going into court and bringing home the convictions is someone else's job. I just handle the appeals, which, as I have said, is a matter of putting pen to paper.

The first case I have been assigned is a horrible, sickening murder. Two eighteen-year-olds, one released from Rikers Island the day before. A burglary off on the wrong foot: someone home. A girl who responded to their knock. They tied her up, wrist to ankle to neck, with her roommate's pantyhose. Filled the bathtub with water, India ink, chlorine bleach; dropped her in, face down. One held her under while the other looked on.

Twenty-nine dollars, a TV that barely worked, a telephone answering machine, a blue duffel bag, a hair dryer, and an alligator purse. The answering machine later sold for fifteen dollars to a Spanish grocer, whose testimony had to be received through an interpreter. Spotted in the vicinity, invited in for questioning, each blamed it on the other. No eyewitnesses, each convicted the other. For me, it's an easy case. Their appeal is frivolous. Except that I looked at the photographs. Don't open the door for anyone, ever.

Three of my stories come back rejected, along with a note: "I will want to read the other two again over the weekend." Time for a little research and evaluation. Who is this guy who writes these coy, provocative little notes?

I have a friend, a former monk, who has a brother-in-law who writes music reviews. According to this brother-in-law, the editor of this little magazine is no small potatoes. Some sort of a bigshot, actually. Formerly the fiction editor of a national magazine with a large circulation and Fortune 500 advertisers, now an editor at a large publishing house, a teacher in the graduate writing program at one of the city universities. A man who has launched careers, changed people's lives. Also somewhat of a writer in his own right, although better known for his other work.

That's all we can say for certain. But out in the wilderness you look for signs. My friend left the monastery when he received the stigmata. Became a shrink. Well, let's see. Based on what he's sent back and what he's kept, it would appear that my correspondent is an anti-Semite. He's not much interested in the ostensibly autobiographical, first-person accounts of growing up Jewish in the Bronx. Meanwhile, he's retained for further study a story written in the voice of an aging Argentine—one of the original, brief pieces—and a longish story, about medieval convent life, a retelling of a tale from the *Decameron.*

It sure wouldn't be a bad thing to break into print with that one. So many pages, not a bad way to get one's foot in the door. My friend, the songwriter, thinks I already have my foot in the door. My girlfriend refuses to hazard a guess. I dare not hope, but I'm more than a little hopeful, actually.

Roy Rogers. I ask a man in the corner, a pack of cigarettes on his table, for a match. He pulls from his pocket a tiny pistol. Pull on the trigger, a flame erupts from the barrel. Funny you should get such a response.

[v]

Eight P.M. It's noisy up here on a Friday night. A lot of smart-looking, well-dressed teenagers having a quick bite in twos and threes before a hot night out. A spotlight shines on the blue and pink banner of the Blue Note, JAZZ capital of the world, a sixteenth note poised in the center, swaying this way and that. The parade of automobile headlights moves slowly west.

Walking here, east on Leroy, between Greenwich and Hudson, there's a schoolyard full of mothers with babies, and an empty swimming pool, dark blue, its still water eerily illuminated by submerged sidelights set into the walls. I bet it would be easy to drown in it. Sixth Avenue is crowded with the usual assortment of dime-a-dozen portrait artists, lined up like cabs at Grand Central, magicians and jugglers, top hats and tank tops, kids queued up early outside the Waverly for the midnight show of *Blue Velvet.* No, this week it's *The Night of the Living Dead.*

The living dead. The dried mustard still yellow, the dried ketchup still red, the photographs still in my head, in living color. You have to wonder: What is it that made them confess? No beatings with rubber hoses, no sleep deprivation, no shady police tactics. Informed of the right to remain silent, of the right to consult with an attorney, informed that anything they said could and would be used against them, they came voluntarily, they came together, two friends, and blamed it on each other. Not a case of a burden of guilt finally too heavy to bear, as in Dostoevsky. Something else.

People must like to run off at the mouth, not realizing the effect of their words. A compliment may insult, an alibi may inculpate. If criminals knew more about criminal law, maybe they would keep their mouths shut. Maybe not. Who knows what goes on in people's heads? Better to say nothing.

The weekend ticked by, the weekend of the rereading, second by second, and on Monday my two stories arrived in the mail, along with a note:

> "I wish that this letter were to be concerned with bet-
> ter than the mere statement that I am extremely inter-
> ested in what you do. I wish I were writing to report
> that I have been persuaded to take either of the at-
> tached, or both. But there we are—and all I can offer
> you is an invitation to keep me abreast of what you are
> up to. Surely you are to be encouraged. But what you
> do not deliver is a degree of wallop that arrives to the

reader out of effect. At all events, I am determined to
keep after you."

An unbroken series of form rejection slips was, all things
considered, easier to take. You come to expect nothing, it's all
right when that's what you get. Better had he said nothing.
He'd drawn me in, offered me a ride. He could have changed
my life. He slammed the door in my face, kindly, gently. I felt
sort of like Grigory Ivanovich, sent out on assignment to the
provinces. But you wouldn't know Grigory; I made him up
and, to compound his regret, never saw him into print.

What did he mean, what was it he was looking for? What
is this thing called "wallop"?

Strange as it may seem, even McDonald's closes at some
point, and people who have never been there at closing time
always seem to find my account of its closing procedures, well,
a little incredible, unworthy of belief. Still, it's true. Quite
abruptly the music goes off, in mid-tune. Searchlights drop
from the ceiling. Sirens sound. The aisles fill with angry mini-
mum-wage, minimum-age employees brandishing broom-
sticks and baseball bats. They're not afraid to use them. That,
I think, is wallop. I gotta go.

[VI]

Once you've ordered the Big Mac, the large fries, and
the large Coke, there's really no excuse. The person taking
your order, as if reading from a script, will prod you: "How
about a hot apple pie today, sir, or ma'am?" What can you do
but say yes.

You get to a certain point, it's too late, you can't go back.
Too late to bask in the glory or the shame of what might have
been eaten but was left, in Styrofoam, on the keep-warm
rack.

I had another story on the back burner, one I'd almost
sent, except that my most honest friends were divided as to its
worth. I placed it in an envelope along with a note:

"Thank you for your kind letter. While I still have your eye, would you mind reading just one more? I wouldn't swear under oath that this one has any more 'wallop' than the others. Nevertheless, I must confess that certain members of my private reading public believe it has 'oomph,' and perhaps that is an acceptable substitute." And then I waited.

In the Book of Exodus were codified the prescribed retributions for various acts considered criminal by the ancient Hebrews. According to Exodus, a man was entitled to kill a thief who broke into his dwelling after nightfall, but was himself answerable in blood to a thief he killed in the daytime. Early English law prescribed the death penalty for the thief who broke and entered a dwelling after the setting of the sun, but spared the life of the thief who committed the same act while the sun was up. The Penal Law of New York makes no distinction between a burglary committed during the day and one committed at night, and in neither case is the crime a capital offense.

Each of my two defendants, to use a phrase much in favor among my coworkers, had "a rap sheet as long as your arm." That's a lot of crimes for a couple of eighteen-year-olds, even measured by a pair of short arms. Mr. James, known to his friends on the street as "Almighty," had once stolen a car, had once been in knowing possession of an unregistered firearm, had on a couple of occasions attempted to rob people on the street at gunpoint but had fled upon encountering resistance, and had broken into a few houses. Mr. Jackson, street name "Sincere," had five burglary convictions to his credit. He had acquired a rack of master keys capable of opening most locks. He would listen at front doors for human voices, animal noises, radio broadcasts, and hearing none, he would walk right in.

December 8, 1985, Tuesday, Sincere knocked on Almighty's door. Mother Almighty let him in. They ate some eggs, drank some chocolate milk. "Let's rob someone," said Almighty. "That's not my thing," said Sincere. "Let's hit a crib."

On the first floor, 1418 New York Avenue, Sincere's keys opened no doors. On the second floor, Sincere's keys opened no doors. The third floor, they knocked, a man answered. "Is Justine in?" "No one here by that name." "Sorry, wrong number." Slam.

Adrenaline flying high, up to the fifth floor, number L–53. All of this, by the way, from Sincere's confession, the more detailed, the more plausible of the two.

Two hard knocks and a girl is at the door. "Yo, Sincere, is this the one?" "No," says Sincere, hiding behind the stairwell. Almighty starts to walk away; the door is still open a crack. "Oh, fuck it!" says Almighty, wheeling about-face, thrusting his sneaker into the crack, overpowering, shoving the door back open, pushing the girl down the foyer. Sincere is right behind.

Fuck it. There's a lot in that six-letter sentence. Her entire future, theirs. Their entire past. Years of rage, years of deprivation, years of petty crime. Six months in, six months out—Rikers Island, the street. It gets old, you get old. Enough is enough, not enough. A lifetime of little break-ins. You want your name in headlines. Fame and fortune, take the bull by the horns, it's not too late, defy fate.

[VII]

I didn't wait long. An embossed return address on the envelope, a single sheet of cream-colored paper, five by seven, and here's what it said, typewritten: "Terrific. I will take it. Will publish at my first opportunity—a year. But not to fret: it's solid, it's certain. Not that I take you to be the fretting sort. Too, I am not ever interested in who the writer is—as citizen. But you provoke an exception. Speak. I am listening with both ears." And a P.S., handwritten: "I want you to show me everything."

. . .

Where's the gold? "I'm not into jewelry." Where's the money? "It's in the eyeglass case, in my room." Let's go. What else you got?

Up here, you can bring your own food. Just buy a cup of coffee or a small soda to establish your credibility as a customer and you're home free. I need to know more about this man, this menace. He may like my stories, but it's me he loves. Obviously. Something's going on here and I don't know what it is. I'd better find out before I reply.

Events are conspiring in my favor, sort of. We are babysitting at my cousin's house. Rows and rows of paperbacks. She has an anthology published in 1980-something and one of his stories is in it. Only five pages, but I can't read it, it's incomprehensible. My wife claims it's a small masterpiece, stylistically similar to my stuff but a whole lot better. We are browsing in the Nine Lives Bookstore. One of his two novels has just been reissued in paperback, but I can't read it. Something about the typeface is hard on the eyes. There's a piece of a column about him in the Books section of *Newsweek.* It seems that he's loved and reviled, that he's a stern taskmaster and a sympathetic listener. My friend's brother-in-law, upon further interrogation, discloses some lurid gossip. Hearsay, inadmissible in a court of law.

I better not take any chances. I opt for spare demographics: "Age: 33. Born: Bronx, New York. Ancestry: Jewish, Russian-Palestinian. Educated: Baltimore and Philadelphia. Occupation: Lawyer. Married, childless."

I am the same age as the original McDonald's franchise. Still young by architectural standards, already an historic landmark.

Both eighteen. Born and raised: Brooklyn, New York. Black. One finished ninth grade; one, eighth. Burglars, killers. Not married, still children themselves.

A slender envelope with the emblem of a New York publisher. A sheet of cream-colored paper, same emblem. "Forty-seven. Lapsed Catholic. Married with children. You are an amazement. I want to see everything." My friend, the former monk, claims that every Christian is an anti-Semite. So be it.

[VIII]

A deep fryer, a microwave oven, a soda dispenser, a shake machine, tin ashtrays, hanging plants. Cash registers, high-schoolers. That's all you need to make a cool million.

A TV set, Zenith, black and white, nineteen-inch. A telephone answering machine, Panasonic, voice-activated. A hair dryer, Remington, built-in timer. A blue duffel bag, twenty-nine dollars, and an alligator purse. That's all there was.

I didn't have a whole lot more myself. Two long things, neither quite right, but each having well-done passages; several shorter things of varying quality and passion; and unfinished bits and pieces. I made some minor additions and deletions to the longer ones and sent them off, along with the best of the shorter ones. "Enclosed is everything—except for a few that I was embarrassed to have read, let alone to have written."

His reply, again on that publishing-house stationery, was immediate. "Your salutations are a little on the formal side, don't you think? It is time we were on a first-name basis. Am I to take it that the work you sent along is all unpublished? You are splendid, but you have a lot to learn. You are young, so you will learn it. I have skimmed everything. Will reread over the course of the weekend. You will please be meanwhile sending me a reply to my question." My adrenaline was sky-high.

But not for long. Those weekends were killers. Calm reflection replaced workaday zeal. The following Monday everything came back. He'd written all over the first couple of pages of each of my stories, but then he'd stopped. And a note:

"Why don't we make a little effort to contrive a time for coffee. I take off for three weeks in two weeks. Possible to give me an hour before then? Nothing here for either my publication or my publisher, but you are for both—and it is this that I want to discuss with you—before it is too late!"

They tied her up, gagged her, and left her wriggling on her bed, like a fish. Filled the bathtub with warm water. Emptied into it bottles of Clorox bleach, India ink. She was an art student. They carried her to the bathroom. "Be careful, don't hit her head," Sincere admonishes Almighty as they place her in the dark pool. A pause. Almighty fixes his clothes while Sincere takes a shit, wipes his ass.

There's a sense that's missing, a lack of method. Why bother to adjust the water temperature? Why worry about banging the head of someone about to be dead? Not too late to change your mind.

Black coffee, white cream. Black men, white bleach. White girl, black ink. Regular bathwater would suffice. There's a symbolism here I can't quite fathom. I doubt even the other Almighty, the divine Author, could know these minds.

White paper, black ink.

[I X]

There is not a McDonald's, not a Burger King, not a Roy Rogers in all of Manhattan that has a pay phone. They all serve salads now, but still no phones. Makes you wonder. Funny thing is, I didn't relish the idea of getting together with this character.

Before all this had happened, I had been an unpublished writer, which wasn't too difficult. Write when you feel like it, succumb to distractions without a second thought. Write about anything that comes into your head, if anything ever does—everything I ever wrote I thought would be my last. The publishing industry was just a form-letter generator. So what. Throw them away with the other junk mail. Dream. Let freedom ring.

But now I was a soon-to-be-published writer and things would not again be so easy. But for one, none of my efforts to date was right. But I was. Now I was really going to have to start churning out the stuff. Where, in the depths of my experience, was I going to find it, and so much of it? I waited a few days, regained my composure. And then I placed the call.

"Mr. Barall, so good to hear from you. I had hoped we could meet before I went on vacation, but it would appear to be impossible. Well, there'll be time later. What kind of law did you say you do?"

"Right now I'm between jobs, actually. But not for long. I'm going to work in the Brooklyn District Attorney's Office in a few weeks."

"When do you manage to write—on the weekends?"

"If then."

"Oh, heavens, how tragic! What can you hope for in your lifetime: a couple of novels and maybe a collection of stories? Well, look, do the best you can and be well. And call me later."

Grigory Ivanovich put out to pasture. Funny what passes for a tragedy in some circles.

"So then Sincere says to me, 'We have to do something with the girl,' and I seen him walking back to the bathroom. Then I knew some real harm was gonna be done to her and I had to get outta there, so I went to wait at the door. I seen him hold her head under the water for about six minutes. Then he came out and said, 'It's all over,' and we wrapped up the stuff and took it to an empty apartment. We looked at the TV for a while and some girls came in. We got into an argument about Sincere killing the girl. At around six-thirty, Sincere went out and sold the telephone machine to a Spanish man in the grocery store."

"I went to wrap up the wires and started putting the things

in the bag. Almighty says, 'We gotta kill her.' I say, 'Why?' 'We just have to.' Next thing, I seen him walking from the kitchen to the bathroom with a mop, and he's using it to keep her head down. This is making me real nervous now, so I started getting ready to go and Almighty comes out and says, 'She's gone.' I ran down the stairs and out the building."

New York Post, page 1: COED MURDERED IN FT. GREENE. Fame, no fortune. Court-appointed defense attorneys. No alibis. Those confessions, no defense.

[x]

In the law, nothing is as easy as at first it looks. My case sure isn't. The Sixth Amendment to the Constitution provides: "In all criminal prosecutions, the accused shall enjoy the right to be confronted with the witnesses against him." The Supreme Court, during the Warren era, in an opinion not yet undone, interpreted this to mean that the confession of one defendant could not be used against the other at trial. In my case, that's exactly what's happened, twice, and it's enough to throw out the convictions—unless. Unless something. Of course, Robert Bork, if confirmed by the Senate, could fix all that.

There must be another way to sustain those convictions, keep these guys in the slammer. The error was harmless beyond a reasonable doubt, because the other evidence of guilt was overwhelming? Hardly. The defendants didn't object vociferously enough to the use of the confessions? They didn't have to. You better hope I think of something, and then write my liberal, bleeding heart out.

[x i]

I am trying a little experiment. Even as we speak, a rivulet of grease is advancing down the table toward me and is staining a light orange color the dam of napkins I've constructed to control its flow. Is pizza fast food? I guess we'll know soon enough.

I was going to tell you about a boy I met on a Coney Island roller coaster. Fast-food places may be good for writing, but nothing is more amusing than an amusement park. Ask John Barth, or Karl. I was going to tell you about this boy. How he went to Princeton to study chemistry, the movements of stray subatomic particles, strangers to the Periodic Table. How he graduated with high honors, went on to Harvard for advanced study, could have gone anywhere. How after four years, after completing all his course work, he was thrown out on his ear. He was a klutz in the laboratory; he just couldn't get his experiments to work out, couldn't get those particles to behave themselves, to behave in accordance with theory. How, down in the dumps, down in the doldrums, his plans fissioned, penniless, he got a job as a lab technician, analyzing water samples for the presence of dioxins. How he started to pick up the pieces. Things were going all right, but they told him he was too slow. How they put him on a quota, ten samples a day, twenty samples a day, how they watched him like a hawk, waited for him to screw up. And then the grant money ran out.

How he came back to New York, went to live at the 92nd Street Y, a stranger among strangers, drifters, people waiting for something to happen. How he found some solace at the Y, organized social outings, made friends, planned trips. How he met a girl who also lived there. His first girlfriend. She didn't think so. How he kept trying to talk to her, she said he was harassing her, she wouldn't listen. How they had words in the lobby and he was banished, told if he ever set foot in there again they'd have him arrested, that's a promise. Banished from the Y.

How he kicked around from one apartment situation to another, driving cabs, selling shoes, darning socks. How he managed to get a job running experiments for some obscure professor at NYU who didn't bother to check his references. How the professor taught him a few basic things about laboratory method so that even his results came out right. How his picture appeared on the front page of the *Times* science section with the professor, who had just been awarded the Nobel Prize, arms around each other.

How the professor wrote a few letters, got him into a doctoral program at Columbia, a subspecialty of a subspecialty that he couldn't even begin to describe, but I could take his word for it, it was a growing field. He was in on the ground floor. How he had a feeling that he had finally turned the corner, that maybe he could still make a decent living and not be a failure. How, with a modest sense of triumph, he had written an article describing these trials of his, which had been published, under a pseudonym, in the *Journal of Humanistic Psychology*.

How he didn't have nice teeth.

How keeping his head above water in that subspecialty required every ounce of his energy and intellect. How, for the five years it took to get the degree, he was permitted only one grade of C. Two Cs and you're out. How, after one year of working like a slave, he already had one, but he still had hope.

How he told me his name, his nickname, his street name, his pseudonym. I remember them all.

I was going to tell you about this boy. But now a blazing orange river is heading right this way and I'm about to be engulfed.

Oh, fuck it. **Q**

"The worth of the critic is known not by his argu-
  ments but by the quality of his choice."

—EZRA POUND

Published as *The Harvard Book of Contemporary American
Poetry,* Helen Vendler's anthology offers readers a list of thirty-
five poets that, according to the book's jacket copy, discrimi-
nates "expertly between the achieved and the merely
attempted." While Vendler presents a body of poetry formida-
ble in its own right, her choice fundamentally distorts the past
fifty years of American poetry's accomplishment.

Vendler's anthology is, in fact, so thoroughly flawed that
one's complaint could begin almost anywhere. Vendler's introduction, for example, has an authoritative air about it, but
proves hollow to anyone at all read in the field. Of Allen
Ginsberg, Vendler writes, condescendingly, that "through the
work of such poets, the poetry of the second half of the century
begins to be ethnically representative." Only the faculty at
teen- and adult-education departments of liberal synagogues,
anxious for attractive course offerings, would think of Ginsberg primarily in that light. Ginsberg, it should be noted,
Vendler also credits with having "found with exhilaration the
proletarian ground cleared by Williams, the first American
poet after Whitman to treat the urban poor in a language
technically appropriate to the subject"; as though it were
enough to choose one's subject strategetically. One can, at least
initially, afford to move quickly over the unfortunate choice of
words, understanding what was meant by "treat the urban
poor," and move on to one of Vendler's more relevant assess-
ments.

The problem with Vendler's approach is that her intelli-
gence is drawn almost exclusively to the "representative" and
never to the gist, so that Ginsberg is valued for having given
voice to a particular segment of the population rather than for
his energy, warmth, rhetorical power, ear, humor, and devel-

opment of the poetic line; Lowell, alongside him, is labeled "the first American poet of the family romance—not the Freudian archetype unadorned, but that archetype tethered by the infinitely many fetters of particular occasions," as though the structure of his verse were of no consequence for our reading. What little is said of Lowell's writing—Vendler mentions "the Poundian heaping up of detail which he marshalled . . . within a magisterial categorical system"—strikes me as misleading.

Vendler *is* capable of reading beyond the lineage and overt subject of a poem, as her general remarks on the Freudian, post-Marxist context of contemporary poetry indicate—but her attitude and principles of selection remain academic in her refusal to assume responsibility for poems as works that are gauged to a respect for the reader's capacity to respond—gauged, in other words, to what Pound called the "quality of emotion," Williams "a machine made of words," and Marianne Moore "a place for the genuine." Nor does Vendler seem at all interested in what Louis Zukofsky called "the range of pleasure poetry affords."

As a result, her anthology champions Stevens, but omits Pound, Williams, Cummings, Stein, Moore, H.D., Eliot, and Crane—none of whom belong, any more than Stevens, in a book of contemporary poetry published in 1985 in the first place. The inclusion of Stevens is defended with the following: "This collection opens with the poetry of Stevens, since he flowered late and came into his own only after the 1955 publication of the *Collected Poems;* he is the chief link between the earlier high modernists and the later poets." In fact, Stevens— who died in 1955—wrote the introduction to Williams's early New Directions *Collected Poems* of the thirties. ("The slightly tobaccoy odor of autumn is perceptible in these pages. Williams is past fifty.") If Vendler were truly concerned with link, influence, and late flowering, the omission of Williams—who published two major books after Stevens's death, and Pound— who sponsored, spurred, checked, explained, and wrote a great deal of what we know today as the best of the century's poetry, would hardly be comprehensible. Along Vendler's line of reasoning, the poems of Emily Dickinson—edited by Thomas Johnson and likewise released in their first complete (untampered with) and therefore newly influential edition in 1955—should also be included.

Vendler's meager defense is far from what one would expect from a critic touted as "the best poetry reviewer in America," and it goes a long way toward obscuring the finer observations in her introduction—her noting, for instance, that "when the history of the relation between the two halves of the twentieth century is written, the second half will be seen, as in the cases of Ammons and Lowell, to be a long critique of the first, as well as a long absorption of it." A contemporary anthology designed to explore that statement alone would be most welcome.

More than twenty years ago, an anthology entitled *A Controversy of Poetry,* edited by Robert Kelly and Paris Leary, approached just such a perspective, albeit inadvertently, as did M. L. Rosenthal's textbook anthology. Neither, in any case, attempted the gerrymandering Vendler engages in—possibly because none of the three had the power actually to change anything on the semiofficial map of American poetry; or, more probably, because all three were able to read American poetry with better discrimination, and—more important—with more faith in the variety of its impulse and in the capabilities of its makers. Set alongside the richness of anthologies such as these, Vendler's is revealed to be shortsighted at best. Had she presented her choice as a volume of "favorite poems," one would perhaps simply leaf through in disbelief and mild regret that a critic of Vendler's stature had so limited and questionable a range of appreciation. Her King of the Hill approach, however, forces one to examine the vision behind her canon making, as well as it highlights the need for a return to a reading of how poems work, not only against other poems, but through their readers.

The distinctly mixed blessing of a home that American poetry seems to have found in the academy is, unfortunately, not likely to foster such an approach, and our poetry's readership, and criticism, needs once again to be put to the test of its independence. Poets such as Allen Tate, Louis Zukofsky, George Oppen, Yvor Winters, William Bronk, Robert Duncan, Delmore Schwartz, Jack Spicer, Lorine Niedecker, J. V. Cunningham, Charles Olson, Alan Dugan, Edwin Denby, Robert Creeley, James Schuyler, Robert Hass, James Tate, and Leslie Scalapino—whose work, as much or more than many of Vendler's selections, accurately reflects the diverse new American reality that Vendler refers to in her introduction, and whom—for the most—the academy has kept on its fringe, are accordingly omitted from Vendler's all too safe and middle-of-the-road gathering. In their stead we get the confused likes of a Michael Blumenthal, who seems to be trying to tickle or charm a poem out of his empty verse:

> I hope you'll forgive the black paint
> on my windows, the smell of cat litter
> in the kitchen. Guests complain sometimes
> that my collection of Minoan cadavers spoils
> their appetite, or that having the shower
> in the living room creates too much moisture,
> but I think you'll grow used to it if we get to be
>   friends.

Of the new writers Vendler does include, Frank Bidart—who isn't represented by his best work—is among the most vital and fully committed to the language of his poems, recording the quiet terror and detail of growth, stasis, and neurosis:

> He's still young—; thirty, but looks younger—
> Or does he? . . . In the eyes and cheeks, tonight
> turning in the mirror, he saw his mother,—

puffy; angry; bewildered . . . Many nights
now, when he stares there, he gets angry:—
something unfulfilled there, something dead
to what he once thought he surely could be—
Now, just the glamor of habits . . .

From "Self Portrait, 1969"

By and large, this new poetry attempts to deal with the visibly or emotionally "real" in straightforward (read lyric, usually first-person) fashion—Charles Simic and Sylvia Plath being the exceptions—but in the cases of Amy Clampitt, Michael Harper, Dave Smith, and Michael Blumenthal, poetry is confused with embellishment or inflation of unintegrated feeling on the one hand—feeling for which there is evidence of neither critical nor temporal responsibility in the poem—and a fundamentally ornamental use of language on the other. In a weak poetry, the relationship between these two factors is inversely proportional: feeling is inflated as the resources of a poet's language are discovered to be incapable of moving the reader; language becomes decorative as the accompanying emotion is found to be slight.

As for the poets Vendler rejects, she writes: "I have had to leave out many poets whose aims were admirable but whose poems seemed thin (whatever their past historical effect)." By "thin" one can only assume she is referring to the "merely attempted"—poems such as Olson's "Cole's Island," Duncan's "Often I Am Permitted to Return to a Meadow," Hass's "Meditation at Lagunitas," Spicer's "A Book of Music," and the like.

One had best call a spade a spade, since Vendler won't, and point out that what she really objects to are poems that extend our notion of the lyric and epic tradition, on the one hand, and poets who adhere to Poundian principles of sound writing on the other. So that a poem like "hmmmm," for example, by Leslie Scalapino, is left out of the anthology, while Amy Clampitt's "A Procession at Candlemas" is included.

hmmmm (from a 28-part sequence)

Haven't I said that part of having intercourse

Haven't I said that part of having intercourse
with anyone is loving them when they are meek
when they can't speak. When a woman, say, mews
(when being flipped over on her belly by a man)
    i.e.
if she utters some sound sort of like what a doll
makes when *it's* flipped forwards. What I mean by
    this
is: her eyelids, after flying open with her head
flipped back, will drop shut when her head is
    forward
And in falsetto (we might even say mawkishly),
the woman's mouth makes a sound like the word
    Mama.

—LESLIE SCALAPINO

. . .

The monk in sheepskin over tucked-up saffron
intoning to a drum becomes the metronome

of one more straggle up Pennsylvania Ave.
in falling snow, a whirl of tenderly
remorseless corpuscles, street gangs

amok among magnolia's pregnant wands,
a stillness at the heart of so much whirling:
beyond the torn integument of childbirth,

sometimes, wrapped like a papoose into a grief
not merely of the ego, you rediscover almost
the rest-in-peace of the placental coracle.

—AMY CLAMPITT

Scalapino's poem takes place in its language, which is put to work within it in order to reveal the poem's subject; so that, in the end, subject and language are, to the close reader, nearly indistinguishable. Judged by Poundian standards, Scalapino's direct treatment of the thing is far superior to that of the Clampitt passage, where, contrastively, one has the feeling that the poem exists beneath its words. Forced and decorative, the language of the poem is pitched too high for what it describes, and the reader is left with the impression of inappropriate strain. Clampitt's line is stiff, usually with iambs, and a fluent rhythm is never engaged. The subject is overtreated, plated with poetic diction. The twist on usage here has little to do with what the poem is after, and the reader is, as it were, browbeaten, rather than carried into, or surprised, or confronted by the language. The poem feels unsteady as a result, though it corresponds to the schoolroom image of a poem as something worked up rather than worked, or given, in a way that Scalapino's obviously doesn't.

The point here is neither that Vendler has been guided by thematic rather than aesthetic concerns (while others would have preferred a standard based on the latter) nor that she has favored one school of poetry at the expense of another, so much as that her selection calls into question her ability to discriminate among poets whose reputations have not already been established by consensus: roughly one third of her selection. It also makes one wonder just how well Vendler did her homework. She notes in her introduction that "as Hugh Kenner reminds us, it is poets—and not anthologists, or professors—who eventually decide which poets are read after their own generation has disappeared." The Harvard anthology would have been significantly different had Vendler looked around more carefully to see which poems other poets were reading before making her choice. As it is, her method of representative selection achieves an absurdity that would find its equivalent in the visual arts with the organization of a show in which Van Gogh is selected for his ability to speak eloquently for the poor, Picasso for his pacifist expressionism, and Jackson Pollock for his having brought the tradition of American Indian sand painting into a contemporary vocabulary; while Matisse is overlooked for his failure to move beyond his preoccupation with line and color onto a major theme, and Rothko is omitted because his work "does not mirror, both formally and in its preoccupation, the absence of the transcendent." Such organization by category is bound both to mislead and to leave fine artists in its wake. Durable poetry, poetry that survives its generation, exerts its power, in part, by defying the sort of easy classification of surfaces that Vendler practices. Vendler's irresponsibility as critical emissary of contemporary American poetry can be traced to her refusal, or inability, to consider the full range of that poetry—"lower limit speech, upper limit music."

The Harvard Book of Contemporary American Poetry is, therefore, something of a ghost town. Having left out a considerable part of what is most contemporary and most American in the poetry of the last several generations, Helen Vendler has produced a lapse that brings to mind a small poem of Jack Gilbert's from the early sixties, "Orpheus in Greenwich Village," likewise excluded from this anthology; its eighties equivalent might have him in Harvard Square.

> What if Orpheus,
> confident in the hard-
> found mastery,
> should go down into Hell?
> Out of the clean light down?
> And then, surrounded
> by the closing beasts,
> and readying his lyre,
> should notice, suddenly,
> they had no ears? **Q**

In the exact measure that he was impoverished, Ye-chetzkell Landau was enriched. To many of the Avenue's on-lookers, Landau was a pitiful figure in his baggy black pants worn threadbare and his white shirts, whose pockets and collars were often torn. On holidays, Landau appeared briefly in the back of the synagogue under the shapeless form of his only suit jacket, a green tweed whose collar tab of mustard felt had uncurled and rolled back into the nape of his neck. Landau's employment during most of the week was to shift behind the counter of a cafeteria—not with quick hands or even an eye for the smack of a pickle under the knife. Knowing customers tried to move their trade down the length of the glass case displaying mounds of ragged corned beef, rolled beef, damp pastrami, heaps of round little tongue slices gleaming with jewels of fat. Yechetzkell Landau's preparations were slow; his assembly of roll, meat, condiment haphazard. Whatever was shouted, "Corned beef on a seeded roll!" "Lean pastrami on pumpernickel!" its opposite was as apt to come over the counter. Glickstein, one owner, kept Landau on only to torment his partner, Glassner.

My father regarded Landau balefully and never let the many occasions slip by to let me know why. An early riser, Dad rousted me out of bed Sunday mornings, holidays, playing Strauss polkas and American marches, fantastic crescendos at six in the morning as Dad twisted the knobs and my mother slept, impervious. My father wanted company along the Avenue, where he made the rounds of cafeteria tables, drumming up clients for a sporadic practice of law. Even on school days, if I turned in the sheets to the tread of shoes on the buckling kitchen linoleum or the teapot whistle on the gas flame, I would find myself urged out the door.

"See Yechetzkell." My father would glower, pointing to the bent back, the greasy shirt, the pants with an uncertain fly seen when the latter was sent out to help bus tables. "A disgrace." In his three-piece woolen suit of blue, holding its press from the cleaners, my father breathed heavily, dramatically. "An ignoramus."

I bowed my head forward to my father's look of disgust, toward the cracked tiles of the floor, scattered cigarette butts, dust balls, scraps of bread, bottle tops.

"*He* has a genius."

I felt my shame, rehearsed so many times—as the idiot, staring off, guileless.

Having spit resentment in the dust, Dad looked up, cheerful, to ask if I wanted a sandwich—corned beef? tongue? It was forbidden food, Mother's ruling, at six in the morning.

There were times when some undertone of worldly amusement in the criminal ran through my father's face as a result of his daily experience with the gamblers, bookmakers, in Dorchester, Mattapan, Roxbury, who could not afford the cost of their crimes and had to come to him for help on credit. Yechetzkell Landau, however, with his gay, rosy smile, oblivious to the wounding remarks of the men and women he served, appeared to radiate innocence. His son—at the head of the class, both in public and in Hebrew school—was a child untouchable by the rest of us. Landau's son spoke only to teachers and to a few special characters. His grades were nearly perfect in elementary school. Hardly a sissy, though, our playmate was known as a familiar of a Dorchester gang of toughs. It was young Landau who told us that Ellen Goldsmith had her pants pulled down behind the fence of the Glenway Creamery. He had seen it, though at a safe distance. What would his father think of this? But Barry Landau's father could not think—his love was uncritical.

"How is your son?" my father would ask, hiding grief, resentment.

"My son?" Yechetzkell Landau would look up, with sweet surprise, from the pumpernickel slice he was mangling. "That boy, you know what he did . . . ?"

I would flee to the men's room while my father had his liver turned on the broiler of the father's epic—*Achievement on Glenway*—which never ended until I was back in sight, Yechetzkell Landau finishing with "And yours?"

"What do you think?" my father whispered, concealing his teeth.

"Wonderful, yes?"

"An idiot."

"No." The counterman's eyes opened wide.

"Yes. The bottom. A disaster."

In his childhood, my father had a reputation as an *illui*. "Genius" is not an adequate translation for its Eastern European context. A genius is a prodigy able to do mathematics, physics, speak languages after glancing at a textbook. A genius goes to school and returns, a curiosity to the neighbors on either side of the fence who knew about him, whereas an *illui* basked in the glow of a whole community of admiring white beards. An *illui* could repeat the abstract logic of talmudic sages and come to original conclusions at seven, eight, nine years old, concentrating upon his diminutive frame the gaze of a town of Jews. Such a glow had my father's boyhood given off—his cousins asserted. My father had mastered English within a year of coming to America, going on to the Boston Latin School, winning prizes easily; then to Harvard, to Harvard Law. Afterward is another story. This is my story.

My story is that my childhood was not distinguished by any glow except the light of my father's discouraged look. There were no prizes until very late, and those I won were dubious, having to do with making noise, not scholarship. And here was Yechetzkell's Barry, a bushy-black-eyebrowed boy, smelling to me of the pickles his father must have slipped into his pants pockets on the way home from the cafeteria, and of the ash barrels of Glenway Street. There Barry could be seen lounging with the five or six well-known delinquents, the children of bookies, of a family intermarried with Irish gangsters, the offspring of runaway husbands, and the funeral director's twins. Barry Landau was the delight of even Mrs. Babbeshevsky, that contagious nervous-breakdown who made me associate ever after the language of the patriarchs with the sound of splitting rulers, shattering chalk, the slamming of books and children against the wall. I paid no attention to the rage of the Holy One with Mrs. Babbeshevsky pounding with her fists on my desk, pulling my hair to get my attention. "You lost your place! You idiot! You lost your place!" I slept in the cave I had heard about, several lessons back in a fragment of translation, next to a shepherd, David. The snapping of the little woman's fingers was but the whirr of bats. When I climbed up for a look around the classroom, there was Barry, borne proudly on her crouching back, her shining rotund flanks, Jerusalemward. That boy's place, my father let me know, was already reserved—at Harvard, no less. And my father now insisted on hearing from the counterman, in the latter's heavily accented English, one by one, the grades, Barry's grades in *cheder,* in public school, subject by subject, while I waited for a sandwich, botched together, and listened to my father pushing rotten eggs—my C's and D's—back across the glass.

My father would watch Yechetzkell cluck to himself, the man looking up to regard me sadly, with such a sense of his own good fortune in his cheek that he narrowly missed adding a thumb to the tongue he was shredding on a roll.

In time, we moved.

We found ourselves out of the crumbling wooden house that had been gerrymandered by carpenters owing legal fees into a three-decker, a cramped bottom floor, our apartment. We went to the brick fronts of Mattapan, where my sister and

I had separate rooms. Yechetzkell, Barry, the agonizing comparisons, were at a distance. Dad was more interested in his own career than in the collapse of genetics, or was temporarily distracted by my sister's relative success in school. Mattapan, too, had its Jewish geniuses—but they had all been skimmed off to the grim blacking factory, the Boston Latin School, while I enjoyed myself, a center of attention, at the local junior-high school, my journeys to my father's bookshelves beginning to bear rewards. When I finally had to enter Boston Latin, in the ninth grade, it was understood that I was only to endure, to pass, no more; the age of expectation was over. It was the era of iron, not of gold. As for Landau, the mention of his name, that of the child from Kerwin Street, or the name of the boy down the block on Fessenden, or of Woodrow Avenue's concert pianist, or the list of the children of bakery assistants, full-grown busboys, janitors, the boys and girls of a generation of slouchers stepping on their own heels, crouching behind their children, who would mount into the sky through the broken window slats, the slack pulleys, the chipped-away putty of their parents' vistas on trash-strewn backyards of Blue Hill Avenue three-deckers—*verboten!* I, too, had grown into the right to a temperament, could slam doors behind me, hide for hours in the bathroom, refuse to return words; and not even a chair hurled would deter my refusal to go on with Hebrew studies that made me feel myself lowered to the lower depths of the unintelligible. It was enough that I had to live through nightmares that extended into the dawn each morning, sadistic masters at the Latin School announcing that it was, at last, all over. I had once too often decisively flunked Greek, flunked Latin, flunked mathematics, flunked even English, one term when the dry grind of doing book reports never to be read aloud, and only occasionally to be graded, pushed me off the deep end of *nolo contendere*.

I rallied.

It was possible with the Irish master.

"Silence, exile, and cunning," though the name of the Dubliner made their lips curdle.

But they understood his slogan well enough. It was the credo of Catholic Boston, which we, the Jewish boys not geniuses but determined to survive, learned quickly. Others gave the answers and we copied, over their shoulders if necessary. We did not belong—fine. Nevertheless, as displaced persons, we clung to seats and obdurately obliged the level of the marks to fall low enough so that we were allowed to go on, lifted by the leveling curve. Among us there was uneasy fellowship. Genius never knows such solidarity of discontent. Anarchists, we shared the knowledge of society as enemy to everyone but the elite. Against authority, revolution is permanent. So dreams go off the rails, the Bolshevik revolution, Cuba, China. Genius is dangerous, often arrogant, leagued with bureau cracy, for which it performs. And genius often turned out to be no more than an aptitude for repetition. In this world, the Landaus do not count. They allow the worst of petty tyrants, the Babbeshevskys, to do their most hideous. The genius does not advance but retards the great movement forward of men and women. Or so I told myself, and grew merry at the counter, seeking out Yechetzkell, relishing the bungled pastrami, answering his "Do you see my boy?"

With "Never."

Answering his "He's busy."

With (inaudible) "Playing with himself."

Landau's name came up in the house no more. My father was too busy with the law to give me much attention—and as a lawyer, he must have been in receipt of disquieting rumors. The bare buttocks of Ellen Goldsmith so lovingly created in stories to my friends and the attempt to penetrate her on the other side by his associates in the gang were but the first buds of Barry's attraction to the buzzing of Dorchester's back lots. Indeed, Barry Landau had ruined Ellen Goldsmith's reputation, and the family moved soon after to Worcester with their daughter. Untouchable because of his perfect grades, Barry went on, with the other geniuses, to poker games on the Nantasket sands, to the pool halls on Talbot and Morton, to the numbers games, the horse races, that precocious status with girls that made their set a class apart at the beach, on the Avenue, at the drugstore corners, fourteen, fifteen, and—finally with their automobile licenses—that sent them completely out of ken the day after their sixteenth birthdays.

I slipped into Harvard—to the Latin School's surprise. The geniuses got an embossed elegant certificate, hand-scrolled, admitting them, while I received a mimeographed sheet notifying me that if I was willing to live at home, I could attend. My father began to believe in luck again, although his law practice started to slide. That is another story, and another, like a wriggling of veins, arteries. I was able to demonstrate, if not genius, a talent for manipulation. At college, I exceeded my father's accomplishments—though, of course, with leisure at my disposal that he never had. I didn't rise at five in the morning to go into the Boston Flower Exchange, hauling cases of wet flowers back and forth at a father's elbow. Nor did I have a stepmother at home, throwing radiators—as a cousin told me, my father discreet on the subject. But this is not a story of success; it is a story of perspective.

I return to the balance of my first sentence. It was provoked by a newspaper article about Barry Landau. His father Yechetzkell—did he ever get to leave the counter on Blue Hill Avenue? Did he shlep out in his worn-away shoes, the backs folded under his heels like a pair of slippers, to the Beverly Hills home of his son?

His son did not go to Harvard. The seat left empty was perhaps the seat that fell to me. Stanford offered a much larger scholarship and, as the top bidder, was first on Landau's list. Later, it would be the Mafia in California, the Teamsters Union, actresses. The cafeteria in Dorchester collapsed, but Yechetzkell was gone by then. Could the father hobnob with hippies, with real-estate sharks, with cocaine-eyed starlets, by the son's poolside, in nylon trunks?

Now, certainly, the father is dead. So is my father.

I crumple the scales in my hand, a newspaper article sent by an anonymous friend: "Attorney Barry Landau . . ." **Q**

As intensely aware members of our society, we despair at the burgeoning irrational fanaticism engulfing modern thought. Gentle paeans of worshipful respect are cruelly thrust aside in favor of blood music. The serene verities of Divine Plan are obscenely mutated and then called fact. The mellifluous concatenation of eternal embrace, the unbounded consecration of piety and purpose, the empyrean beatification of the vulgar multitudes ARE truly wrought! Sacerdotal acolytes seeking their vocation through a honed edge of revered steel, holy metal, holy mettle, drain their carmine essence as blessed baptism upon the soils of the victor to assure the harvest of fertile bounties of God's love. This is indeed a small price exacted by God's priesthood, ennobled haustellate mendicants, for such searing luminosity!

As you slake the fulminating appetites of fiat deities' bootstrapped avatars by offering your children purged of the loathsome bacchanalia of material defilement, bodies girded to carry the Pearl of Great Price, they are denied their earned emplacement within the pantheon of the righteous by involuntary chemical transformation! Secular humanists have infiltrated the clinics where breeding women are controlled and, in nutritionist's guise, have polluted the sanctified essence of our children, babies in the womb, with thiamine.

THIAMINE! Thiamine pyrophosphate ("pyro" means "hellfire") is added to bread, insinuating into the bodies of your children, infiltrating their innocent flesh, crassly challenging the inerrant correctness of thought of all good men! This ravening perversion extrudes its unctuous vermiform phallus to thrust deep within our babies' viscera, disgorging stinking miasmic ichor, strewing excrement in the aseptic corridors of a child's soul. Thiamine's molecules harbor the sulfur of acid rain, the nitrogen of NO_x smog, and the filthy black carbon of poisonous carbon monoxide. Thiamine reduces your angelic children to vicious manifestations of oozing putrescence, befouling and ulcerating the virgin innocence in which God quenches his thirsty love.

The lizard nutritionist slides in his slime in the shadows, poison dripping from fangs and acid dripping from claws, reptilian scales glistening in dappled obscurity, waiting to chemically transform your children beyond your embrace, beyond your very reach! Sentinel at the portal to extermination, to oblivion, to a writhing, screaming plunge into the steaming, stinking abscess of secular humanism, the nutritionist waits for your children with infinite patience and niacin.

NIACIN! Sweep away the jeweled cloak of niacin and see nicotinic acid in God's bright light! It is born of nicotine, from tobacco, through the very same oxidative chemistry that rots your garbage and creates fire to inflict agony upon the fallen! Niacin is the liquid poison nicotine distilled from tobacco and rendered by the Fires of Hell to be secreted within the food of your innocent children.

The distilled hellfire essence of tobacco is in the white bread of your little children. Does your child cry? Does your child shriek? Does your child scream? Does your child cry and shriek and scream with the unending blowtorch agony of nicotinic acid burning though his gut, tearing his mind into bloody shards, forever estranging him from the jealous, incorruptible compassion of omnibeneficent God? Is it already too late?

Open your eyes and see the secular humanist floating beneath the stagnant green pool, maggots squirming in the unspeakable corruption upon his back, film-covered eyes balefully surveying the next victim slated for chemical transformation. Contamination! Pollution! Anathema! The nutritionist, humid armpits exuding the rank stench of the corridors of hell, greedily lusts for the immaculate soul of your child, unmasked and unmaskable as the snake in the Garden. Evil demands feeding and fattens within the wasting flesh of your loved ones!

The purchased souls of government enforcement coyly turn their heads and smile behind modestly placed hands, contemplating profit without measure, quietly delivered and quietly accepted. Watch as the nutritionist plunges his mottled yellow fangs deep into your baby's skull, sucking out the multicolored jelly as you scream and scream and . . .

VITAMIN E, alpha tocopherol, is the vicious unguent that enrages beyond human control the animalistic sexual frenzy of your little babies in their cribs. Alpha tocopherol is the slippery exudate of pernicious lust goading the monomaniacal orality of your little children, compelling them to lick and mouth any object they may grasp. The death of Freud and the birth of alpha tocopherol occupied the same five-year span! This diseased essence of slithering infantile sexuality came to be extracted from a being of unbounded saliromania into a chemical of ultimate lascivious deviation!

Listen to your babies unendingly cry in their perpetual agony as they cruelly slip forever beyond God's limitless compassion. They scream outrage in the obscene denial of control of their divinely bestowed sanitary bodily functions, to be fouled victims of the felonious fortification of all they consume, to worship the darkness, "E" before "I," the alpha without the omega, alpha tocopherol, Vitamin E!

Listen to the secular humanist chortle and snigger while swallowing gobbets of phlegm and spurting viscid spews rankly steaming in God's clear air. Detect the nutritionist shielded by the courts and emboldened by the legislatures, slipping pyridoxine into the flesh of your babies.

PYRIDOXINE! Its sound does not fit the human mouth! Pyridoxine is the prurient exudate isolated from ungodly vats of yeast slime owned and operated by those who would with microbiological excrement smear God's love in the Black Mass celebration of genes and chromosomes. As maggots gambol

within the liquefying flesh of an aging corpse, so does pyridoxine fester the living substance of your own beloved children.
Your living gift to God is chemically transformed into fuel to
fire the furnaces of hell!

Ponder the cumulative effects of a decade of pyridoxine
toxification. View the skin of your young teenagers as it
decomposes before your eyes, disgorging pus and miasma,
splitting like the rind of an overripe fruit saturated to bursting
with the loathsome products of some dreadful fermentation.
View their bodies as rank animal hair forces its way through
their skin and the fetid odors of the damned pool about them.
These profane atrocities are your children! Disfigured and
defiled, wracked by bestial appetites, seeking further debase-
ment with an unquenchable pestilential fervor, your babies are
a fleeting source of amusement for the nutritionist seeking
unendingly greater damnations.

Do you doubt? Look at your milk cartons. Wantonly pro-
claimed by government mandate and backed by the frightful
armed might of the military is Vitamin D milk. Vitamin
DAMNED! Calciferol, Vitamin Damned, is chemically created by
irradiation of God's immaculately conceived ergosterol
through a pericyclic rearrangement conserving orbital symme-
try. Listen to the nutritionist howl with delight. Watch ulcer-
ous crimson pustules erupting from thick folds of cheesy white
dermis ooze a clotted yellow pus perfumed with the cloying
sweetness of rotted flesh. His wet red fists clench a bulging
gunnysack convulsing with twisted souls. Your children stalk
you with chemicals in their eyes, blood music in their minds,
souls screaming with the perpetual agony of the damned! Your
tongue squirms over your clenched teeth, growing more raw
and more bloody and more diseased as you chant the rasping
threnody of hell!

Today we retch with the cinereous despair of scientific
nutrition filling our mouths. Now vile and bitter gall burns in
our throats as we strangle upon scientifically formulated sin!
The obese torpor of the secular humanist, edematous body

exuding sheaths of billowing mucus dribbling down turgid extremities to puddle in stinking pools, gives way to lecherous frenzy at the opportunity to stoke the furnaces of hell with shriven souls! Your babies are alien abominations distorted beyond humanity by the synchronous megahertz chant of reeking monolithic circuitry, computers watchfully charting their descent into the abyss. The nutritionist has been summoned to plunge his festering putrid fingers through your child's eyes, deep into his brain, to squeeze the soft mass into a dripping pulp and punch his gushing fist through your baby's skull.

Humble piety, the sweet song, the gentle, swift susurrus of whispered prayers punctuating the ripening of thought and purpose, the approach to literal understanding—this was the daily worship of thinking, subservient men. How we exulted in that holy purpose! What light and power could be obtained through unquestioning obedience, a triumph of will, to those who had personally forsworn all ambition that they might serve as the self-appointed direct embodiment of God's will on earth. How many of us floated in the bright, bright, inerrant truth, in fealty serving. As individuals and as the invincible clenched fist of a nation we were content to satisfy God's ravening hunger to His greater glory.

Will you acquiesce to the concupiscent deviation of your children's lives from the honorable field? Will you shun the luminous pleasure of God's wynd? Will you allow the evolutionary vitaminification of America to chemically transform your pellucid, fluid adoration of the Creator into some viscous, rancid, and loathsome avocation? Have you eaten of this bitter fruit? Where will YOU stand when the heavens split asunder? Where will YOU be on that Judgment Day?

Pathetic sinner, who will save you now? **Q**

Michael and I always sit close to each other. We sit on his long, low couch watching his giant television set. He has a plaid blanket over his knees like an old man keeping warm on the deck of a cruise ship. "Will they do that to me?" he asks. "Lock me up?" He strokes the back of my hand with his pale, freckled fingers. Michael sees his family, pious with prayer, armed with Bibles, marching off the farmlands, then locking him away. "Probably," I say. Michael is thirty. He says he will die when he is thirty-three. Like Christ and Tom Dooley. Michael wants me to be still and listen to him dying. "Hear my heart," he says, putting my hand on his chest. "It's so slow," he says. His heart skips beats beneath my hand. "It's jumping from drugs," I tell him. Michael's house is full of drugs and money and a small, bronze statue of a bent naked man giving birth, baby's head forcing itself into life through the tip of the penis. Cowboy made Michael the statue. Cowboy is passed out in the bedroom. I love Cowboy. Cowboy loves Michael. They are lovers. Michael loves everybody. As I watch Michael's pale hands, I think of Cowboy's hands. They can do everything. I love men's hands. They are the sexiest part of men. Cowboy is not my lover, but he knows my body better than any lover. By trade, Cowboy is a masseur. When he touches my body, in a dim room, while strange music plays, I lie very still and want to say, "Oh, my beloved, my beloved, please." Those lines belong to somebody else. I forget just who. Cowboy combs my hair, polishes my nails and toenails. He knows when I look ugly. Somewhere safe in the suburbs stays my family. Tomorrow I return to them, like a package mailed from another country, damaged in shipment. Sunday house will be empty. My family will be at the country club golfing. In the yard I have planted a garden. Tomatoes, green beans, peppers, and chives, surrounded by marigolds to protect them. I will pick tomatoes and chives for salad, roast chicken with lemon and butter. Bake bread with wheat germ. Years ago someone told me, "Happy women bake bread." I knew he was nuts. Down in the duck pond swim two ducks. Duck lovers stay together for life, I have read. In the middle of the pond, on a small island, a giant willow droops and dies. All I love is here, and I am afraid in this yard. I feel safest with Michael and Cowboy. Last night Michael throws a big party, rents half a hotel. Early evening, while Cowboy is dressing, I go down to the bar, meet some football players on a famous Midwestern team. I know their coach. I sold him a car. The hotel is half faggot, half jock. There is no difference. They have seen my friends. "Where are your pretty boys?" The football players laugh. I think of two boys I went with in high school, Moose and Oats. Football players, boys I went steady with to protect me from the girls. They wanted to make love, but they were so clumsy, their hands heavy like big hammers. I did their homework instead. "Would you like to have dinner with us?" the famous players ask. "With some real men?" Cowboy comes in bar. His dark hair curls around his face. Looks to me like an angel boy painted by Caravaggio. Cowboy is tall but looks half size next to the football players. "This is my friend," I say. "He's a carpenter." He's that, too. He makes tables and chairs. Ordinary things. The football players nod, uneasy. The party is everywhere. I am surrounded by beautiful men who don't like me. Cowboy goes to dance. Michael and I stand in the corner and watch. "You don't love him," I accuse Michael. Michael laughs. Michael puts the vial to my nose and the rest of the evening is lost. Except I remember thinking this is something like hell; if I go now I won't have to go later. **Q**

I flew over to Vancouver from Nelson to go to the New Poetics Colloquium because I had to be in Vancouver anyway, to read for the Pat Lowther Award benefit, and also because most of the writers I knew were going to be at the colloquium. People die and leave their diaries behind; that's why I'm afraid of flying. I'm afraid I'll die in a plane crash and everybody will read my diaries, things like:

> Worked in yard. Not too many phone calls. Thinking abt. Andrew and wondering why he's not showing up. Caroline and I went to caber-tossing; she taped pipe band.

When I get off planes, I feel as if I've been held at gunpoint for several hours and then let go, an escape; it's always miraculous. The New Poetics Colloquium was being held at the Emily Carr School of Art on Granville Island and there, behind Granville Market, out on the dock, having lunch and talking theory, were all the women from the conference. They were mostly Americans, and I listened and tried to understand some of the theory. I couldn't keep up with it. I was sitting beside Pauline Butling and she said she couldn't keep up with the theory, either. One woman from the States said something about "the nature of my experience." I thought, I should write down what the nature of her experience is, but that's all I remember. I really wanted to get to know them, but they were all talking vitally and intensely to each other.

"There's a lot of Americans at this conference," said Pauline.

After sixteen years in Canada, I wondered if the Americans would recognize me as an American.

"Are they saying content is important or not important?" I asked Pauline.

"Well, I don't know really," Pauline said.

I love Granville Island. There are so many city people out having outrageous fun in the outdoors, it makes you want to weep. It's a strange little exciting sort of Disneyland for Yuppies. I wish I could live there and drink young beer forever. Or for at least one week.

A woman from San Francisco was breast-feeding a baby at the same time she was discussing theory in the most amazingly abstract terms. I don't know why the women all ended up together. How does this happen? Will somebody do a study? Street buskers were playing and singing all over the market area. There were two jugglers named Dick and Dick, who had drawn a huge crowd and were yelling things like "And now we will start throwing these razor-sharp juggling clubs!"

So I went back when the talks started up again. It appeared that the women were pissed off at the men. The men talked about deconstruction and poetics and said things about lineation. The women went for coffee together and spoke about pagination and lineation and discourse and absorption.

Dick and Dick were back again, hustling the crowd, passing a paper bag for the money. It was an exceptional day; big ripped-looking clouds were getting torn off eastwards, and the sailboats were banging themselves in the masthead with those giant marine snap-shackles. What a great day to sit out on the dock and drink wine, with Dick and Dick yelling, "Don't applaud now, folks, SAVE THAT APPLAUSE!" and then, *"Now! Now!"*

The men, I think, were all somewhere else together, both American and Canadian deconstructionists, continuing to say theoretical things to one another, and Dick and Dick were screaming, "We will soon be appearing in Calgary by special request of the VANCOUVER CHIEF OF POLICE!"

It was exhausting, really.

The conference was sponsored by the Kootenay School of Writing, and they had worked for months to obtain the funding and get it all set up, and everything was going smoothly, I suppose. Most of the poetry confirmed and illustrated the theory of deconstructing language. I wonder, If you write deconstructionist poetry very strictly according to theory, if you could, without either brains or talent, appear to have both? Maybe so. Deconstructivist poetry is very democratic.

The major speaker was Charles Berstein, an American, who is what you might call one of your main Deconstructionist Men. He can talk deconstructionist talk for hours. Berstein said really, really complex things. I couldn't understand them. I mean I could not understand two sentences in a row. But it was a beautiful day to be on Granville Island, what with Dick and Dick, and wine, and I was pissed off that Andrew hadn't shown up. He said he was stuck in Frobisher Bay on a shoot. Oh, if only my friend Andrew could see me among all these deconstructionists, I thought. I'm so cute when I'm confused. However, breakthroughs in literature can only grow out of a fertile field of audacious failures. And funding. I could see that most of the speakers at this conference lived on the Planet of the Grants. They lived on Funding World.

The upstairs lecture hall at Emily Carr was full mostly of men—men lecturing and men in the audience. I went down and watched Dick and Dick for an hour. They were a perfect team. "And now as a protest against traffic lights, we will . . . SET OUR CLUBS ON FIRE!"

They do all this stuff in double-voicing, and they really did set their clubs on fire, flaming torches orbiting their heads in figure-eights. There was also inviting, exotic music coming from the big, covered market. It sounded as if you could take your false self out to dinner in there and buy it anything it wanted.

Back at Emily Carr, Nicole Brossard got up and said that women had to develop their own feminist theory of writing, and ignore the men. Ignore the men, she said, and do your own thing. Or something like that. I had to ask somebody again because of my extremely short attention span.

"What'd she say about content?" I asked Angela Hryniuk. "Did she talk about whether content is important or not?"

"Well, I'm not sure," said Angela. "But she's really good. She's inspiring."

Angela Hryniuk used to be a student at David Thompson University Centre in Nelson; there were a lot of former DTUC students at the colloquium, most of whom had last been seen on the road out of Nelson, with mattresses and bicycles, heading toward Vancouver, in search of an education.

I am extremely short on poetic theory, and often I don't think I'll ever write poetry again; sometimes literature is surrounded by a large dense cloud of gentility. If I get funny, I thought, I'll end up laughing by myself. It's the practice of extinguishing a response by non-acknowledgment. If you run into something funny, just don't laugh. Glare.

At the break, I went and asked Colin Browne if I could crash at his place. But he said he was full up, and pointed out to me another guy, named George, who had room and an extra foamie. George had a girlfriend, Alanna, who was an exotic dancer and whom I knew from the year before at the Women and Words Conference, where she had done a belly dance during performance night and where a lot of the women had been offended.

Joan Webb was also in town. She's a writer who lives in the top half of the house I live in, in Nelson. She's not a belly dancer. Anyway, Joan and I walked around, looking for one of Vancouver's famed secondhand clothing stores so I could buy something to wear to the reading the next day.

"So what are the women deconstructionists saying?" I asked Joan.

"Hell, I don't know," Joan said. "There was this one woman who had some poem about desire for the *object*. I think she meant penis. One of the others gave her a hard time about it afterward, and she said, 'I'm not molesting you, am I?' I mean, she used the word *molest* for *bother.* It was weird."

We found a secondhand store and went in to play in the rags.

"Actually, I'm interested in it all," said Joan.

There was an orange silk skirt and a big top to go with it. I don't think I look good in orange.

"Oh, yes, you do," said the saleswoman. "It's your color."

"But I'm a winter," I said.

The skirt looked kind of like a sarong, and the top was gigantic and hung all over me.

"Winters can have oranges," the saleswoman said.

Joan found a pair of earrings that were tiny pistols in holsters.

That afternoon, they told me there was another good speech; the American woman with the baby had spoken and so had some other people. By the time the talks were over, it was dark and everybody was full of energy from sitting around all day. Angela Hryniuk, Steve Fearing, Sandy Duncan, Joan Webb, Kathy Armstrong, and I were trying to find Steve's car, so that we could all go to the party and get drunk or something.

"Well, what were some of the great things people said?" I said.

"It was all titters," said Joan Webb. "People weren't laughing with their bodies."

I began to understand that there's something about deconstructionist poetry that makes people want to lay back. Maybe they're Buddhists. When you deconstruct language, what you end up with is deconstructed language. It's like deconstructing a cat—what you end up with is a dead cat.

"So did they say anything about content?"

(One last try.)

"It's their conference," said Joan Webb. "They can *not* talk about anything they want." **Q**

I came to the city and discovered everyone discussing Rimbaud.

Once a year, I leave the forest in order to assess the progress of civilization. I travel to a nearby metropolis, walk the streets, glance at the papers (until nausea overcomes me), strike up conversations where I can. It is not a happy exercise; it is a duty. But surprise and delight overcame me when I heard that name on so many lips.

Rimbaud! The *enfant terrible* of nineteenth-century French poetry. What had suddenly attracted Americans to him? What astounding shift in national sensibility had made a hero out of a poet? But then I thought, Why not? Was there not something quintessentially American in his character? His rejection of authority, which set him wandering like a French Huck Finn. His support of the underdog—see him at the barricades of the Paris Commune. His restlessness, searching out the frontiers of Western culture. His independence, imagination, and egotism: these had demanded a new literature, a new life. Yes, there was much to admire.

And it hinted at a pattern, at a revitalizing and uplifting of the entire society. Perhaps the day was coming when I would once again dare to live in the world. After all, the year before, the popular mind had fastened on Mozart.

I approached a young fellow on the street and asked him how he had first learned about the poet.

"Rimbaud!" (He incorrectly stressed the first syllable, but I was willing to make allowances.) "The movie, man, the movie."

Yes, I was right: just like Mozart. Apparently Hollywood was using some of its awesome power to raise the aesthetic understanding of the masses. No doubt the producers had built their story around certain melodramatic incidents: the first flight and imprisonment, the street battles in Paris, the violent quarrels with Verlaine. And on his youth, the American obsession. This was what tied the two together: Mozart composing symphonies at eight, Rimbaud penning masterful verse at fourteen. I pardoned it, if it led beyond the artist to the art itself.

I inquired further, whether the film included the encounters with the Parnassians, the escapades in London, the shooting in Brussels.

"No, man, in the jungle, in 'Nam."

The jungle? Vietnam? Not what I expected. True, at the age of twenty-one, Rimbaud had, in despair, given up literature and gone East: as a Dutch soldier to Java, as a coffee trader to Arabia, as a gun merchant to Ethiopia. But I had not known he had visited Indochina.

I should have known. **Q**

The firebox in your gut, white-hot, driving your legs like pistons—*she is sleeping with that bastard*! Christ, it's black out—your feet are soaked—sand? In the middle of a lawn? You stumble over a rake—grass underfoot again—the Impala may have seized up three miles back, but this sure as hell won't! You whack the .45 automatic in your back pocket, which is half dragging your jeans down. Five more miles to Millerton? Ten? You'd make it on bloody stumps—the door to her apartment (fake Colonial brass knocker glimmering like a grail before your vision) ripped from its fake Colonial hinges—Pow! Pow! Pow! You grin at the amazement on Ernie Burr's face, a hole the size of an orange in it through which you could see the stars—if there were any tonight—a *clean* hole, the kind Fearless Fosdick shot in people! You laugh wildly, the sound ricocheting off like a horse neighing—that conniving, unprincipled, two-timing bastard Burr—*and she can't deny him.* I can't help myself, Alex, she tells you, it's bigger than both of us—legs churning, babbling into the black, suddenly you're airborne.

"I beg your pardon," offers a calm, deep voice, so close you scramble onto your knees in fright. "Profoundest regrets," it continues. "You encountered my equipage." A gray shape detaches from the general black velvet, looms over you. "Might I offer you a support up?"

Your eyes must be getting used to the dark—he wears high boots, over the knees, and a huge coat, or cloak, that reaches almost to the ground; and his hair, standing out from his head like a ballerina's tutu, is so white it glows.

"I am George Washington," he says. He is holding a golf club. You get up.

"I'm on my way to Millerton," you say. "My girlfriend is

sleeping—this minute—with a son of a bitch whose brains are going to be scattered over Connecticut!" You don't mean to say so much, but you can't contain it. You jerk out the .45 and wave it.

"I like this game," the guy in the cloak says. "I trust I am getting better at it."

You notice what you'd tripped over—a huge leather golf bag. The guy is sighting along his club as if it's a rifle. Ahead, up a slight rise, is the suggestion of a green's disk with a white flag to left of center, and the pale grin of a sand trap wrapping around to the right. The man is now addressing the ball, an aspirin in the grass at his boots.

"A 9 iron?" erupts out of you unbidden. "For Chrissake, that's a hundred and fifty yards—" and you are pulling the 5 out of the bag (there's no 6 iron), wooden-shafted with a queer bell-shaped blade and a soft silver glow. "I caddied all through high school," you offer somewhat apologetically, handing him the club.

"Much obliged," he says. "The set is a gift from Revere."

"What the hell is going on?" You squint at the dial of your Timex. "Nearly 2:00 A.M.—golfing—in that getup!"

He has his big hands wrapped around the shaft in a base-ball grip, concentrating on the ball. "And why are you here?" he inquires, now looking up toward the flag.

You're holding the gun like a stubby pointer. "My piece of shit called an Impala broke down—she is sleeping with that—blackguard—I'm bushwhacking to Millerton in order to—to—" Beholding Ernie Burr's sly features, you squeeze, two shots ratchet up.

"Ah . . ." says Washington, and returns his attention to the ball.

The hit is surprisingly easy to follow, like a lightning bug arcing through the dark. It lands thirty feet above the pin, just off the apron.

"On in four," he remarks thoughtfully, handing you the club.

243

You sheathe it, shoulder the bag, heavy as rocks, and follow him. You want to see what he'll do with this putt; the green is a crêpe with convolutions. Besides, it's on your way.

It seems to have grown lighter, maybe the moon coming up behind the clouds, because you can see him pretty clearly. He stands with arms folded, one booted foot stuck forward, staring down at the ball as if it were a map of Yorktown.

"Don't let me arrest your march upon Millerton," he says. "I am one acquainted with the concept of timing."

Thirty-plus feet to the pin: five of apron, a twenty-degree pitch with ten-degree drop left for about fifteen feet, then the line crosses at forty-five degrees a foot-high wave over a buried drainpipe, levels briefly, and rises in a reverse twenty-degree tilt to the cup.

"You'll need a computer for that one," you murmur.

Washington nods solemnly. He is big in moonlight. As he squats to study the line of march of ball to pin, his cloak flares and he looks like a steel-gray cone topped with a dab of whipped cream.

He stands and accepts the silver-headed putter (shaped like a flattened lady's slipper, engraved with scenes of battle—horse, cannon, musket). He stances over the ball, shifting in his great boots as though settling down through muck onto bedrock. The moon throws his shadow away toward the lake. The white flag with the red 4 on it stands against the deep blue sky scattered with back-scattered light. Washington smiles, a smile as enigmatic as the dollar bill's. The club, his only living thing, moves and the ball starts soundlessly; neither hurrying nor tarrying, rolling down an invisible track toward, as the pros say, its appointment with destiny. Following the vectors of this man's calculation, the ball rolls and rolls (you feel the clothes sagging on you with night-damp); rolls down the broad green tongue of grass like a white mouse, over the ground swell, rolls and rolls. You and he waiting, silvered cast of Colonial golfer and caddy; she waiting spread breathless in Millerton; Burr hanging there up above her, silo door open and Minuteman poised, waiting. The ball entering now its final motion, rising and slowing, slower (the .45 hangs dead metallic), slower . . . until you realize, with a shiver, it has rimmed the cup and stopped. Hangs there like a crumb of whitest cake.

You turn to Washington. He opens his gloved hands in a small gesture, retaining the putter.

You gather up his equipage and he takes it. He mounts the horse, which you hadn't noticed, a big white fellow he must get around the golf course on. They look like a statue you've seen somewhere, maybe the picture of a statue, except the statue didn't have a golf bag. He touches finger to forehead, and the horse wheels and moves away uphill, sprightly, toward the fifth tee, white hocks rising and falling. **Q**

Those were the years of the Ginger Rogers–Fred Astaire movies, and since his mother and father loved to dance, the three of them saw every movie as soon as it opened.

After the movie, they would go to Jacobson's for ice-cream sodas or hot chocolate, depending on the season. While his parents argued about the dance steps, he would sit quietly and suck up all the soda at the bottom of his glass, or tip his head back and hold his cup as nearly vertical as possible and let the last drops of hot chocolate run down its side into his mouth, until his mother noticed and told him to stop.

At home, his mother and father would turn on the radio and try out the dance steps they had seen in the movie. When the music ended, his father would draw his mother close and hold her for a moment and try to kiss her.

"Remember Little Big Eyes," she would say in a warning tone as she pulled away.

He knew that Little Big Eyes meant himself, and he guessed that hugging and kissing were wrong, or that it was wrong for him to see them; he did not know which.

On summer evenings, he liked to dance with the flowers on the white hydrangea bush in the back yard. It was so tall, and its branches spread so far, that it was more of a small tree than a bush. He did his best to dance with all the flowers, even those at the top. Stretching up on tiptoe, he pulled the branches within his reach, as close to him as they would come, and took them into his arms. Then he swayed back and forth, leaning his cheek on the flowers and nuzzling them against his shoulder, feeling the coolness of their white faces.

He tried to hum the music he heard at the movies and on the radio, the music his mother and father and Ginger Rogers and Fred Astaire danced to. Or he made up his own songs, humming aloud while he tenderly waltzed the flowers as far as they could move, which was not very far, since they were bound into the thick main stem, almost a trunk, that drove down into the ground.

He liked to crawl into the cool, dark chamber formed by the spreading branches, particularly in the afternoon when the sun was high and it was too hot to dance. He would sit with his back resting against the main stem, and watch the sunlight shifting across the grass, and think about how he would have a house and a yard and a white hydrangea bush when he grew up.

When he grew up, he did in fact have a house and a yard and a white hydrangea bush. Even as an elderly man, he went on taking care of the lawn and the flowers himself, just as his father had done.

In the fall, he trimmed the hydrangea. Reaching in among the torn and withered leaves, he cut off the faded flowers and threw them over the backs of the lawn chairs until he had time to dispose of them properly.

By then they were speckled with reddish-brown flecks and had turned a pea-green color. Stroking their heads, he was surprised that they still felt as fresh and cool as they had in their summer whiteness. Their heads hanging over the edge of the chair backs, the flowers lay languid in a way that made him think of fragile ladies at court, spent and sated with dance, their green brocade gowns loosened at the throat as they opened their mouths and sought the air.

After he died, his wife and daughter would cut the dead flowers when the season turned. His wife would cut off the ones on the lower branches. Then she would call his daughter, who would take his favorite cutters off the nail on the garage wall and cut off the flowers at the top of the bush while her mother stood waiting to receive them. **Q**

They
giggled
constantly

Rice © 88